South of the Sahara

Annurin fiska kaurin hanji
A shining face goes with a full belly.

South of the Sahara

Elizabeth A. Jackson

Fantail

Hollis, New Hampshire

First printing January 1999
Second printing June 1999

All photographs and art work are by Paul Quinn unless otherwise noted.
Black and white line drawings are based on artwork featured in *African Designs from Traditional Sources*.
Proverbs are Hausa with English translations.

Library of Congress Catalog Card Number: 98-70505

ISBN   0-9655209-6-X

Published by:
Fantail
P.O. Box 462
Hollis, NH 03049
http://www.fantail.com

Table of Contents

photo by Thadd Jackson

Nigerian woman with calabash of sorghum at Yadakunya

Introduction

West Africa stretches in a wide band southward from the harsh sands of the Sahara Desert to the warm and humid coasts of the Atlantic Ocean. Since ancient times traders traveled the dusty routes across the desert to exchange salt and spices for gold, ivory and slaves in the south. Powerful empires such as Ghana, Mali, Songhai and Kanem-Bornu rose at the gates of the desert where they grew rich controlling the trans-Saharan trade. For many years this trade was the only interaction West Africa had with the rest of the world.

In the fifteenth century the Turks blocked the overland trade route to Asia, and Europeans began to search for a way around the African continent. Portuguese ships were the first to come ashore on the coast of West Africa. It did not take long for them, and the rest of Europe, to discover the wealth this new land offered. The Portuguese, French, British and Scandinavians built forts along the coast and used them to stockpile gold, timber, ivory, cocoa and of course slaves, ready to ship back to their homelands. The mighty northern empires of West Africa declined as the focus of trade shifted away from them.

Slave trade was outlawed in the early nineteenth century, and the Europeans began to venture further inland in search of resources to replace it. In 1884 most of West Africa was divided up between the French, British and Portuguese. The region lived under artificial boundaries and various policies of colonial rule until West African countries began to gain their independence starting in 1957. The modern countries, from Senegal in the west to Nigeria in the east, still reflect colonial boundaries. Some ethnic groups have been divided, and some have been forced to live together under one government. Today, many of these countries are still trying to sort out their identities.

The West African coast is a humid and swampy stretch of land. Some countries such as Liberia and Sierra Leone have a monsoon climate with heavy rainfall. Seafood and coconut palms are plentiful. Inland are thick rainforests, which gradually open onto grasslands. Yams can grow as large as one hundred pounds here. Cassava, cocoyams, kola nuts, and many vegetables are cultivated. Tropical fruits and wild game are abundant. Further north in the true savannah the country is drier, and millet or sorghum are grown in place of yams. Groundnuts are an important crop in this region. The baobab trees spread their weird branches across the flat horizon. Fulani nomads drive herds of cattle over the savannah, bringing meat and milk to villagers in exchange for grains.

North of the savannah the parched and sandy Sahel lies on the outer fringes of the Sahara. In this desert climate water and food are scarce. This is the world of the Tuareg, fierce desert traders and warriors.

Today West African food products are available even in snowy New England. Nearly every major city has at least one small grocery store selling some African products. Tropical fruits and yams have become commonplace on grocery store shelves.

West African cooking requires very little specialized equipment. You will need either a food processor, blender, or grinder in place of the large mortar and pestle that African women use to pound their grains, beans and vegetables. A heavy cast iron or non-stick pot is useful for cooking fufu and some of the rice dishes. This same pot can be used for frying, along with a deep fat thermometer.

The beauty of West African cooking is its flexibility. There may be dozens of variations for a single dish, and you can easily tailor that same dish to suit your tastes. Traditionally a sauce would be made with whatever was available on that particular day. Meats, seafood, leafy greens and spices are easily substituted, increased or decreased.

8

West African Countries Today

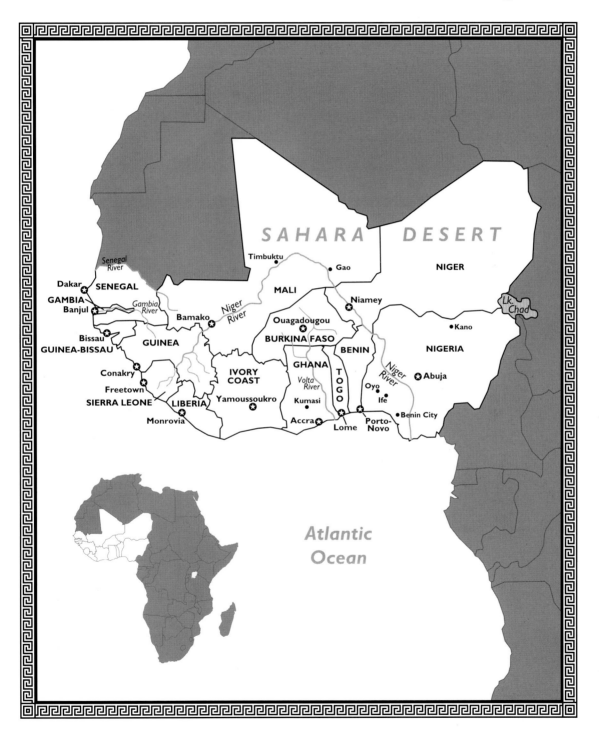

SAHARA DESERT

Timbuktu

Gao

NIGER

Senegal
River

Dakar

SENEGAL

MALI

Niamey

GAMBIA

Banjul

Gambia
River

Bamako

Niger
River

Ouagadougou

Lk.
Chad

Kano

Bissau

GUINEA-BISSAU

GUINEA

BURKINA FASO

BENIN

NIGERIA

Conakry

IVORY
COAST

GHANA

Volta
River

TOGO

Niger
River

Oyo

Ife

Abuja

Freetown

SIERRA LEONE

LIBERIA

Yamoussoukro

Kumasi

Benin City

Monrovia

Accra

Lome

Porto-
Novo

Atlantic
Ocean

This book grew from a desire to taste again the spicy and exotic foods I remember as a child growing up in West Africa. You probably can understand the longing for something you once enjoyed but can no longer find, or can not remember how to make. Nearly everyone has experienced a flood of memories brought on by a smell or taste passing your lips for the first time in many years.

Whether you are rediscovering West African foods, or experiencing them for the first time, this book will be your guide. Perhaps you have sampled the foods of Morocco, Ethiopia, Kenya, Egypt or South Africa. Now it is time to take a journey south of the Sahara for some of the most exciting and memorable dishes you will ever taste.

A baobab tree against the West African horizon.

Cool Drinks

Ginger beer with sugar cane swizzlers

Palm wine is a drink as old as West Africa itself. For centuries men along the coasts and forests of West Africa have tapped the trunk of the palm, gathered and fermented the sap. In the farming regions to the north grains such as millet are fermented into a potent drink. The beverages featured in this section are much lighter, and you can still drive home after you drink them. They are simply cool and refreshing, to quench your thirst on a hot day or extinguish the fire of a spicy West African meal.

Contents

photo by Thadd Jackson

Yellow Bird eating cashew fruit. A single nut hangs at the bottom of each fruit.

Nunnane daya ya fi dari danya.

One ripe fruit is better than a hundred unripe.

Chapman

Today, a traveler in a West African city such as Kano might decide to step in out of the intense heat to an air-conditioned lounge for a relaxing drink. Very likely it will be a chapman, a citrusy drink with a touch of bitters. Garnished with large chunks of tropical fruit, it is the ultimate refreshment on a hot day.

2 tablespoons squash (see recipes in this section)
3 to 4 drops aromatic bitters, such as angostura
1 bottle bitter lemon (you can substitute Sprite if bitter lemon is not available)

1. Measure squash into bottom of a tall glass.
2. Add bitters.
3. Fill glass with sprite or bitter lemon. Garnish with chunks of tropical fruit and serve chilled.

Yield: 1 chapman

Note: Bitters are sold in liquor stores, the mixed drink section of a supermarket, or by mail order. (See Sources)

Ginger Beer

This cold yet burning drink tingles with excitement! Plan to let it sit at room temperature for at least a day before chilling it in the refrigerator.

½ pound (250 grams) fresh ginger
2 limes
1½ cups (300 grams) sugar
½ teaspoon cream of tartar
½ gallon (8 cups/2 scant liters) boiling water
½ teaspoon baking yeast

1. Wash, and then grind or grate ginger, peel and all. Place in large bowl or pitcher.
2. Juice the limes and add the lime juice along with the peels, sugar and cream of tartar to the ginger.
3. Pour boiling water over ginger mixture. Leave about two hours, stirring occasionally, until it has cooled to room temperature. Make sure water is no warmer than body temperature before beginning step 4, or the yeast will die.
4. Strain into a pitcher, and sprinkle yeast over top. Leave about five minutes to soften yeast, then stir. Cover and leave at room temperature 24 hours.
5. Strain again, chill and serve.

Yield: ½ gallon (8 cups/2 scant liters)

Note: See photo on page 11.

Lemon-Lime Squash

Squash is a concentrated fruit syrup which is mixed with water or soda. Fresh squeezed citrus juices are best for making squash. The sweet and sour combination is a perfect thirst quencher.

1 cup (200 grams) sugar
¼ cup (60 milliliters) freshly squeezed lemon juice (1 lemon)
¼ cup (60 milliliters) freshly squeezed lime juice (2 limes)

1. Mix sugar, ½ cup (120 milliliters) water, lemon and lime juice in a small saucepan. Bring mixture to a boil over medium-high heat. Remove from heat, and cool to room temperature.
2. Store squash in a tightly covered jar in the refrigerator until ready to use.
3. When ready to serve, combine ¼ cup (60 milliliters) squash with 1 cup (240 milliliters) cold water (or a mixture of 1 part squash, 4 parts water) in a tall glass. Serve chilled, or with ice.

Yield: 1½ cups (360 milliliters) squash

Orange-Lemon Squash

Orange-lemon squash has a milder flavour than the preceding lemon-lime recipe. The fresh squeezed juices are made into a concentrated syrup to be mixed with cold water or soda.

1 cup (200 grams) sugar
½ cup (120 milliliters) fresh squeezed orange juice (2 oranges)
¼ cup (60 milliliters) fresh squeezed lemon juice (1 lemon)

1. Mix sugar, orange juice and lemon juice in a small saucepan. Bring mixture to a boil over medium-high heat. Remove from heat, and cool to room temperature.
2. Store squash in a tightly covered jar in the refrigerator until ready to use.
3. When ready to serve, combine ¼ cup (60 milliliters) squash with 1 cup (240 milliliters) cold water (or a mixture of 1 part squash, 4 parts water) in a tall glass. Serve chilled, or with ice.

Yield: 1¼ cups (300 milliliters) squash

Pineapple Spice Drink

This spicy and fruity drink can help take the edge off a hot day. Begin preparations a day ahead as you need to refrigerate it for at least 12 hours.

1 large pineapple, leaves removed
½ teaspoon whole cloves or ¼ teaspoon ground cloves
1 cup (200 grams) sugar
1 teaspoon ground ginger or 3 (2-inch) pieces ginger root, peeled and coarsely chopped
8 cups (2 liters) boiling water

1. Slice pineapple (peel, core and all) into thin slices.
2. Combine pineapple slices with cloves, sugar and ginger in a bowl or pitcher large enough to hold one gallon.
3. Pour boiling water over mixture. Stir to distribute spices. Cover and refrigerate at least 12 hours, and up to a day.
4. Strain mixture into a pitcher, and discard pineapple slices.

Yield: ½ gallon (2 scant liters)

Guava Nectar

If you are lucky enough to have fresh guavas you can make this nectar for a refreshing drink, or as an ingredient for the guava sorbet in the dessert section.

1 pound (500 grams) ripe guavas
1 cup (200 grams) sugar

1. Wash guavas and cut in chunks. Mix fruit with 3 cups (725 milliliters) water and the sugar in a large saucepan. Bring to a boil, and simmer 10 to 15 minutes. Remove from heat.
2. Allow juice to cool, and strain through a sieve. Store in refrigerator.

Yield: 4 cups nectar

Ancient Empires: Ghana

Hundreds of years ago, around 300 A.D, the North African Berbers gained control of the land below the desert which linked the Sahara to West Africa. They began to tax the dusty camel caravans that exchanged goods between the worlds above and below the desert. The upper Senegal River valley, rich with gold, fell into their kingdom. *Kaya Maga*, or the Gold King, ruled at the beginning of the empire of Ghana.

The Soninke from south of the desert took control of Ghana about 400 years later. From the capital city of Koumbi-Saleh, they ruled an ever-expanding territory straddling two desert passageways. Moroccans traveled along the northern route, and the eastern roads brought Africans from Kanem, Lake Chad, and as far as the Nile. Camels arrived loaded with copper, dried fruit and cowries. The most valuable of the goods, traded for its weight in gold, was salt. When the caravans wound their way back through the desert, besides the gold, they took slaves, ivory, kola nuts, gum and cotton.

In the 11th century an Arab historian wrote about his travels in sub-Saharan Africa. He noted that the King of Ghana lived in a palace built of stone and wood with glass windows. An army of 200,000 warriors protected the land, including 40,000 archers. In the lavish royal court, guard dogs wore golden collars, and one king tethered his horse to a gold nugget.

The Berbers who originally controlled Ghana also led to the country's demise. By the end of the 11th century, Ghana was weakened by raids from the desert. The ferocious Sosso people gained power in the early 13th century. According to legend, this clan of Malinké blacksmiths was led by the powerful magician Sumaguru. He did not rule the country for long, however. In 1240 Sundiata destroyed the remains of Ghana, and began to rule over Mali, the next great West African empire.

Kowa ya rena gajere bai taka kunama ba ne.

He who despises that which is short has not trodden on a scorpion.

Small Chop

Corn cakes

West Africans traditionally eat one large meal each day and supplement it with snacks, known as small chop. There are many fried or steamed delicacies from which to choose. Stroll the streets and markets of any major city or small town and you will find men selling corn and tsire roasted over coals, women with painted metal bowls full of steaming, peppery black-eyed pea fritters just out of the hot oil, or children with trays piled with plantains, biscuits or fried millet cookies. Throngs of street vendors offer soda, candy or gum to go with your traveling smorgasbord.

Contents

Chin loma ya fi jiran malmala
Eating a mouthful is better than waiting for a helping.

Skinning Black-eyed Peas

Loosen skins by crushing peas slightly with a rolling pin, or a potato masher. Rub the peas between your hands firmly to remove the skins. Rinse in a large pot, swirling water around in a circular motion and letting the skins rise to the top, then letting them float off when you drain the water. Continue rubbing the peas between your hands and rinsing until all the skins are removed. This task is less tedious if you give yourself plenty of time. It is a great excuse to listen to your favorite music or catch up on a TV show.

Black-eyed pea fritters (kosai or akara)

How to Fry Foods

The most important part of frying is having your oil at the correct temperature. It should be hot enough to quickly cook the outer layer of the food, forming a barrier that prevents your food from soaking up oil. If you are deep frying, you must use a deep fry-candy thermometer. They do not cost much and are worth the investment. The oil should reach the temperature specified in the recipe before you drop in the food. When you shallow fry, with only an inch or so of oil in the pan, there will not be room for a thermometer. Just take a small piece of food or batter and drop it into the oil. When it sizzles and begins to turn brown your oil is hot enough to begin.

Fry your food in batches, so that they are not touching each other in the pan. After each batch is removed, take the time to let your oil heat back up to the proper temperature before you put in another batch. During this time you can scoop out any broken bits of food with a slotted spoon and dispose of them.

Make sure your pan has deep sides to avoid splattering oil over your kitchen. This also gives you a place to attach the thermometer. Your pan should be made of a heavy material that will hold heat well. Cast iron is perfect for frying.

Frying foods should not be a rush job. Do not wait until your guests are seated at the table. Start well ahead of time. You can always set the table or prepare other food while the fritters are bubbling away in the oil. Fried food usually needs a few minutes to cool down, anyway.

After you finish frying, just leave the oil in the pan to cool completely before disposing of it. Depending on what you made, you can strain it into a jar and keep it for another use, or discard it. If you were frying a very strong food such as fish, or something that made the oil foam, discard the oil. Some foods, such as black-eyed pea fritters, actually improve in colour and flavour when you use the oil a second or third time.

Fried plantains with egg and savory rice cakes

Black-eyed Pea Fritters

These golden fritters are a staple of West African cuisine. In southern Nigeria they are called akara, but in the Hausaland further north they are kosai. There will always be women in the market place or village with a pot of oil, frying kosai. On a crisp and sunny African morning, or anywhere in the world, this is the best breakfast that you can have. Be sure to leave plenty of time for this recipe. You will need to soak the peas overnight, and removing the skins can take a good half hour of your time. Then you will need to let the batter set for several hours or overnight. I usually start this dish one or two days before I intend to serve it.

    1½ cups (300 grams) dried black-eyed peas
    2 onions, coarsely chopped
    1 teaspoon ground red pepper (more or less to taste)
    1 to 2 tablespoons chopped fresh red peppers
    ½ teaspoon salt
    4 cups (1 liter) peanut or palm oil, or a mixture of both

1. Soak black-eyed peas overnight. Drain. Remove skins (see Skinning black-eyed peas on page 24).
2. Combine peas, onion, ground and fresh red pepper and salt in a food processor or blender. Process until very smooth. Add 4 to 6 tablespoons of water if necessary. You should not feel any lumps when you rub mixture between your fingers.
3. Let the batter sit for at least 8 hours, and refrigerate overnight if possible. It will become frothy.
4. Heat oil in large, heavy pot to 360°F (180°C). Stir batter vigorously to remove air bubbles. Drop batter into oil in large spoonfuls, a few at a time, and fry until golden, about 4 minutes per side. Continue frying in batches. Drain on paper towels. These fritters are equally good served hot or at room temperature.

Yield: 10 to 15 fritters

Note: See photo on page 24.

Spicy Plantain Bites

Brown and crispy on the outside and soft in the middle, these bites are similar to spicy home fried potatoes They make a wonderful topping for groundnut chop. Make sure your plantains are completely yellow before using them in this recipe.

   2 plantains, ripe but still firm
   2 teaspoons ground ginger
   1 teaspoon ground red pepper
   1 teaspoon salt
   1 tablespoon lemon juice
   1 cup (240 milliliters) peanut oil

1. Peel plantains by cutting through the peel lengthwise with a sharp knife several times, and sliding fingers under the peel to remove. Cut plantains in quarters lengthwise, and then into ½-inch (1½ centimeter) cubes.
2. Combine ginger, red pepper and salt in a small bowl.
3. Toss plantain cubes with lemon juice in a larger bowl. Add spices and toss to coat.
4. Heat oil in heavy pot or skillet until a plantain cube dropped in the oil sizzles and begins to brown. Add all of the plantains, turning gently with spatula. Fry until golden on all sides. Drain on paper towels.

Yield: 2 cups, enough to serve as a topping for groundnut chop

Note: You can substitute 1 tablespoon yaji (page 187) for the ginger, red pepper and salt.

Corn Cakes

These round, crunchy snacks are fragrant with onions and red pepper. Serve them with a spicy dipping sauce.

1 cup (150 grams) yellow cornmeal
⅓ cup (50 grams) white flour
1 teaspoon baking powder
½ teaspoon salt
½ teaspoon ground red pepper
1 tablespoon sugar
2 eggs, beaten
1 small onion, finely minced
2 tablespoons water
4 cups (1 liter) vegetable oil for frying

1. Combine cornmeal, flour, baking powder, salt, red pepper and sugar in a medium bowl.
2. Add eggs and onion, and mix well. Add water and mix to form a stiff dough.
3. Roll dough into small balls about 1 inch (2½ centimeters) in diameter.
4. Heat oil in a deep, heavy pot to 360°F (180°C). Drop balls in oil and fry until golden, about 4 to 5 minutes for each batch. Drain on paper towels.

Yield: 15 to 20 corn cakes

Note: See photo on page 21.

Fried Plantains with Egg

The egg makes a savory coating which complements the sweetness of the plantains in these bite-size snacks.

2 ripe plantains (yellow with black spots)
1 egg
1 cup (140 grams) flour
1 cup (240 milliliters) vegetable oil
salt to sprinkle

1. Peel plantains by cutting through the peel lengthwise several times, and sliding fingers under the peel to remove. Slice into ½-inch (1½ centimeter) rounds.
2. Beat egg in a small bowl. Measure flour into another bowl.
3. Heat oil in a heavy skillet until a drop of egg sizzles when dropped in.
4. Dip plantain slices in flour, then in egg, and then in flour again. Drop slices into oil, working in batches so that they are not crowded in the pan. Fry on both sides until golden, turning with tongs. Drain on paper towels.
5. Sprinkle with salt before serving.

Yield: 3 cups

Note: See photo on page 25.

Fried Yam Balls with Corned Beef

This is comfort food – soft and mild with the flavour of beef to balance the starch. If you want it a little less comfortable, you can increase the amount of ground red pepper.

> **1 cup (240 milliliters) cooked and mashed yams (See step 1 below for cooking and mashing yams)**
> **1 egg**
> **1 small onion, finely chopped**
> **½ teaspoon salt**
> **¼ teaspoon ground red pepper**
> **¼ cup corned beef, chopped or crumbled**
> **4 cups (1 liter) vegetable oil**

1. One average 3-pound (1½ kilogram) yam will yield 3 to 4 cups of mashed yam. Peel yam with a sharp knife, and cut into ½-inch chunks. Cover with water in a saucepan and simmer until yam is very soft, at least 30 minutes. Mash in a large sturdy bowl with a potato masher or heavy spoon. Do not purée in food processor or blender, as this will make the yam too watery. You can use yam flour or fufu mix for this recipe as well, by combining the mix with enough water to make a soft dough.
2. Combine 1 cup mashed yam, egg, onion, salt, red pepper and corned beef in a large bowl. Mix well.
3. Heat oil to 375°F (190°C) in a deep, heavy pot.
4. Roll batter into balls about 1 inch (2½ centimeters) in diameter. They will be very moist. Drop balls into hot oil. Fry in batches without crowding, about 8 minutes per batch, until golden brown all over. Remove and drain on paper towels.

Yield: 12 yam balls

Golden Plantain Cakes

These golden cakes with a crunchy outer layer are called tatale in Ghana. Ripe plantain has a sweet flavour which blends with the spices to satisfy all of your senses. Make sure your plantains are very ripe – they should be completely yellow with black spots.

2 very ripe plantains
1 onion, coarsely chopped
¾ cup (120 grams) yellow cornmeal
½ teaspoon ginger
½ teaspoon ground red pepper
½ teaspoon salt
5 tablespoons peanut oil
1 tablespoon palm oil, or 1 extra tablespoon peanut oil

1. Peel plantains by cutting through the peel lengthwise with a sharp knife several times, and sliding fingers under the peel to remove. Slice in large chunks. Combine plantain and onion in food processor or blender and process until smooth. Or, you can mash plantain, mince onion finely and mix these two together.
2. Combine cornmeal, ginger, red pepper, and salt with plantains. Mix well.
3. Heat oils in heavy skillet until a small drop of plantain mixture sizzles and begins to turn brown. Flatten a piece of batter the size of a golf ball into a flat cake. Fry cakes in batches until golden brown on both sides. Drain on paper towels. Serve warm.

Yield: 20 cakes

Puff-puffs

Round and rich with raisins, puff-puffs taste like a fluffy fried scone.

> 1½ cups (200 grams) white flour
> 2 teaspoons baking powder
> 1 tablespoon cold butter
> 2 large eggs
> ¼ cup (60 milliliters) milk
> 2 tablespoons sugar
> ½ teaspoon vanilla
> 2 tablespoons raisins
> 4 cups (1 liter) vegetable oil for frying
> powdered sugar for dipping

1. Mix flour and baking powder in a medium bowl. Cut in butter with a pastry blender until it is the size of small peas.
2. Beat eggs, milk, sugar, vanilla and raisins together in a separate bowl.
3. Stir flour mixture into egg mixture. The batter will be stiff.
4. Heat oil in a deep, heavy pot to 360°F (180°C). Scoop up clumps of batter, about 1½ inches (4 centimeters) wide, and drop into oil. Fry about 6 at a time, for 5 minutes each batch, turning once during frying. Remove and drain on paper towels. Serve warm, with a bowl of powdered sugar for dipping.

Yield: 15 puffs

Puff-puffs

Plantain fritters

Plantain Fritters

Soft, sweet and peppery, these fritters bring out the best of the plantain. Make sure your plantains are very ripe – they should be completely yellow and beginning to turn black – or they will not mash easily.

2 ripe plantains
1 egg
½ cup (120 milliliters) milk
1½ cups (200 grams) white flour
⅓ cup (75 grams) sugar
2 teaspoons baking powder
¼ teaspoon salt
¼ teaspoon ground red pepper
4 cups (1 liter) vegetable oil for frying

1. Peel plantains by cutting lengthwise through the peel with a sharp knife and sliding fingers under peel to remove. Cut into several large pieces. Purée plantain pieces, egg, and milk in a food processor or blender. Or, you can mash plantain with a fork and mix with egg and milk.
2. Mix flour, sugar, baking powder, salt and red pepper in a large bowl.
3. Stir plantain mixture into dry ingredients, mixing only until moist. Do not beat. Let batter sit for 10 to 15 minutes.
4. Meanwhile, heat oil in deep, heavy pot until it reaches 360°F (180°C). Drop batter by large spoonfuls into hot oil. Fry about 2 minutes per side, or until golden brown. Drain on paper towels and serve warm.

Yield: 20 to 25 fritters

Note: See photo on page 33.

Koro-koro

These thin, crunchy cornsticks twist into interesting shapes as they fry. They make a striking complement to a spicy soup or stew.

1 cup (150 grams) yellow cornmeal
2 tablespoons sugar
¾ cup (100 grams) white flour
1 egg
4 cups (1 liter) vegetable oil for frying

1. Mix cornmeal, sugar and flour together in a medium bowl.
2. Whisk egg with ½ cup (120 milliliters) water in a separate bowl. Combine with cornmeal mixture and knead several times to make a stiff dough. Let the dough stand 30 minutes at room temperature.
3. Roll a small bit of dough between your hands until it is as thick as a pencil and about 5 inches (12½ centimeters) long. Continue to roll strands of various lengths. Sometimes you can connect the ends to make a ring. A variety of sizes and shapes makes this dish look appealing. Lay koro-koro out on a baking sheet as you make them. It is easiest to roll all the dough out before you begin to fry, since it can stick to your hands.
4. Heat oil to 360°F (180°C). Fry strands in batches, turning once, about 3 minutes per batch, until golden. Remove and drain on paper towels.

Yield: About 35 koro-koro

Note: See photo on page 60.

Savory Rice Cakes

These crunchy cakes have a slightly firmer texture than potato pancakes. Use a short grained (sticky or glutinous) variety of rice.

> 1 cup (200 grams) short-grain white rice
> 1 egg, beaten
> 1 small onion or two scallions, finely minced
> ½ teaspoon salt
> ¼ teaspoon ground red pepper
> ⅔ cup (100 grams) all purpose white flour
> ½ cup (100 grams) minced, cooked meat or fish, or cooked chopped tomatoes and okra
> 1 cup (250 milliliters) vegetable oil

1. In a large saucepan, combine rice with 2½ cups (600 milliliters) of water. Bring to a boil, lower heat and simmer, covered, until rice is very soft and water is absorbed, about 20 to 25 minutes. Beat occasionally with a wooden spoon during cooking. Transfer rice to a large bowl and let it cool slightly.
2. Add egg, onion, salt, ground red pepper, flour and minced meat, fish or vegetables to the rice. Stir until thoroughly blended.
3. Heat oil in a heavy skillet until a small drop of batter sizzles when you drop it in the oil. With floured hands, shape large tablespoons of batter into flat, thin pancakes about 3 inches (7½ centimeters) across. Coat with flour and carefully lower into oil. Fry 3 cakes at a time. Lift gently from bottom of pan with a spatula if they are sticking, and turn at least once during frying. Fry on each side 3 to 5 minutes, until golden. Remove with a slotted spoon. Drain on paper towels. Continue with remaining batter, frying in small batches until all of batter is used.

Yield: 10 rice cakes

Note: See photo on page 25.

Sweet Rice Cakes

This sweetened version of the crunchy rice cake may be too heavy to serve after a meal, but it makes a wonderful snack or breakfast treat. A short grained (sticky or glutinous) type of rice works best for this recipe.

    1 cup (200 grams) short-grain white rice
    1 egg, beaten
    2 tablespoons sugar
    2 tablespoons grated fresh coconut
    ¹/₈ teaspoon nutmeg
    ²/₃ cup (90 grams) all purpose white flour
    1 cup (240 milliliters) vegetable oil

1. Combine rice with 2½ cups (600 milliliters) water in a large saucepan. Bring to a boil, lower heat and simmer, covered, until rice is soft and water is absorbed, about 20 to 25 minutes. Beat occasionally with a wooden spoon during cooking. Transfer rice to a large bowl and allow to cool slightly.
2. Add egg, sugar, coconut, nutmeg and flour to the rice. Stir until thoroughly blended.
3. Heat oil in a heavy skillet until a small drop of batter sizzles when you drop it in the oil. With floured hands, shape large tablespoons of batter into flat, thin pancakes about 3 inches (7½ centimeters) across. Coat with flour and carefully lower into hot oil. Fry 3 cakes at a time. Lift gently from bottom of pan with a spatula if they are sticking, and turn at least once during frying. Fry on each side 3 to 5 minutes, until golden. Remove with a slotted spoon and drain on paper towels. Continue with remaining batter, frying in small batches until all of batter is used.

Yield: 10 rice cakes

Note: See photo on page 25.

Ancient Empires: Mali

Kangaba was a small town that splintered off from Ghana as the empire was breaking up. When Sumaguru of Sosso overthrew Ghana, he assassinated all the sons of the ruling family of Kangaba. Only one child was spared; little Sundiata was considered too weak and frail to be a threat to the kingdom. This child grew to be a powerful warrior who avenged his family and brought the Empire of Mali to power. Along with the gold trade, Sundiata encouraged agriculture. The farming of sorghum and millet thrived during his reign from 1230 to 1255 AD.

Sundiata's grandson and successor was Mansa Kankan Musa, a devout Muslim who built up the universities of Mali. Mansa Musa made a famous pilgrimage to Mecca, accompanied by 60,000 followers and 80 camels loaded with gold. On his way home he stopped for a long visit to Egypt, spending lavishly and impressing everyone there with his wealth of gold.

The city of Timbuktu began as a Tuareg camp, just at the close of the Ghanaian Empire, in the 12th century. Tuaregs moved south to stay at the camp during the dry season each year. When they returned to the desert, the camp was put in charge of an old woman named Buktu. Timbuktu literally means "the place of Buktu" in the Tuareg language. The camp at the desert crossroads grew to become a town and then a large city, attracting traders and Muslim scholars. The University of Sankore was built there by an architect who returned with Mansa Musa from his famous pilgrimage.

Mali began to decline in the 15th century due to internal fighting and raids from the surrounding people such as the Mossi and Songhai. Gradually the great empire was reduced to a small settlement on the Niger river, just the way it had begun. Today, the Malinké descendants live in Senegal, Mali, Guinea Bissau, Ivory Coast and The Gambia.

Yunwa ita ta kan maida yaro tsofo, koshi shi ya kan maida tsofo yaro.
Hunger makes a youngster old, repletion makes an old man young.

Steaming with Cornhusks and Banana Leaves

Cornhusks and banana leaves make a fantastic wrapping for steamed foods such as the dumplings featured in this cookbook. Please note that they are not edible wrappings! Cornhusks are sold dry, and you will need to soak them in water for about an hour just before using them. If banana leaves are stiff you can roll them up and steam them for 20 minutes. Frozen and thawed banana leaves should already be pliable enough to use.

Tear some of the smaller husks or pieces of leaf into strips about ½ inch (1½ centimeters) wide to use as ties. You will need to tie two cornhusk strips together to make a longer strip. Make up as many of these as the recipe yield calls for, and a few extra.

Banana leaves are very long, and come in sections which may measure 3 or 4 feet. Tear them along the grain into 6-inch (15 centimeter) sections. Cornhusks only need to be spread out, but try to use the larger ones for wrapping.

Place the amount of filling called for in your recipe in the center of the wrap, and fold the shorter ends over the center, overlapping one another. Fold the longer ends inward about ½ inch one or two times, and then fold both ends over until they meet in the center. Use the strips you made earlier to tie each packet around the middle.

Continue to make packets until all of your filling is used. Steam as directed in the recipe. A vegetable steamer spread out in a large pot works well.

Steamed black-eyed pea dumplings (moyin-moyin)

Steamed rice dumplings

Steamed Black-eyed Pea Dumplings

Southern Nigerians call this firm, spicy dumpling moyin-moyin. You will need to soak the peas overnight, and removing the skins can take a good half hour of your time. You can do this up to two days ahead. After the skins are removed, refrigerate the peas until you are ready to begin the dish.

1½ cups (300 grams) dried black-eyed peas
1 onion
1 tablespoon tomato paste
1 teaspoon ground red pepper
½ teaspoon salt
½ cup (120 milliliters) peanut oil
1 tablespoon ground crayfish (optional)
½ teaspoon curry powder
1 teaspoon Maggi Sauce or daddawa

1. Soak black-eyed peas overnight. Drain. Remove skins (see Skinning black-eyed peas on page 24).
2. Combine peas, onion, tomato paste, red pepper and salt in a food processor or blender and process until completely smooth. Add 4 to 6 tablespoons of water if necessary. You should not feel any lumps when you rub mixture between your fingers.
3. Stir oil, ground crayfish, curry powder and Maggi Sauce into pea mixture.
4. Wrap dumplings in corn husks or banana leaves according to method on page 39. Place 2 large heaping tablespoons, or about ¼ cup of mixture in each leaf. You can also wrap dumplings in 6-inch (15 centimeter) squares of aluminum foil.
5. Place a steamer rack in a large pot and add water just to bottom of rack. Place packets on rack, and bring water to boil. Simmer over low heat, covered, 45 minutes.

Yield: 10 dumplings

Note: Maggi Sauce can be found in the soup section of most grocery stores, or by mail order (see Sources). If Maggi Sauce is not available substitute a liquid bouillon.

Steamed Rice Dumplings

You can dress up this mild rice flavour as much as you want by adding more hot peppers, palm oil, or any of the optional ingredients. The easiest way to eat this soft dumpling is with a spoon, right from the wrapping.

1 cup (180 grams) Cream of Rice instant cereal
1½ cup (360 milliliters) boiling water
2 hot red peppers, seeded and minced
1 onion, minced
1 teaspoon salt
3 tablespoons peanut or palm oil

Optional ingredients: ¼ pound (125 grams) chopped, cooked shrimp; 1 teaspoon ground crayfish, 1 chopped tomato

1. Measure rice cereal into a large bowl and pour the boiling water over it. Stir vigorously until the water is absorbed and the mixture is smooth and stiff.
2. Add red pepper, onion, salt, oil and any optional ingredients and mix well.
3. Wrap dumplings in corn husks or banana leaves according to method on page 39. Place ¼ cup of the rice mixture in each leaf. You can also wrap dumplings in 6-inch (15 centimeter) squares of aluminum foil.
4. Place ¼ cup (60 milliliters) of rice mixture on each foil or leaf, fold ends over and seal to make a packet.
5. Place a steamer rack in a large pot, and fill with water just to bottom of rack. Place packets on rack, bring water to a boil, and steam 20 minutes.

Yield: 10 dumplings

Note: See photo on page 40.

Steamed Egusi and Black-eyed Pea Dumplings

Egusi (pronounced ee-goosey) gives these spicy dumplings a nutty taste. If egusi is not available you can substitute sesame seed meal. Be sure to leave time to soak the peas overnight, and remove the skins. You can do this up to two days before preparing the dish.

½ cup (100 grams) dried black-eyed peas
1 onion, coarsely chopped
¼ teaspoon ground red pepper
½ teaspoon salt
1 cup (140 grams) egusi

1. Soak black-eyed peas overnight. Drain. Remove skins (see Skinning black-eyed peas on page 24).
2. Combine peas, onion, red pepper, and salt in food processor or blender. Process until very smooth. Add 1 to 2 tablespoons of water if necessary. You should not feel any small lumps when you rub mixture between your fingers.
3. Stir in egusi.
4. Wrap dumplings in corn husks or banana leaves according to method on page 39. Place a large tablespoonful of pea mixture in each leaf. You can also wrap dumplings in 6-inch (15 centimeter) squares of aluminum foil.
5. Place a steamer rack in a large pot, and fill with water just to bottom of rack. Place packets on rack. Cover and bring to a boil. Simmer 30 minutes. Serve dumplings warm.

Yield: 8 dumplings

Fancy Terrine of Black-eyed Peas

This savory loaf is layered with black-eyed pea purée, meats, seafood, hardboiled eggs and vegetables. It is filling enough to make a meal, or an elegant addition to a buffet or cocktail party table – truly worthy of the name Nigerians use to describe it – rich moyin-moyin. It is best to purée the peas just before you assemble the loaf.

For Purée:

2 cups (400 grams) dried black-eyed peas
1 onion, coarsely chopped
1 tablespoon tomato paste
1 teaspoon ground red pepper
½ teaspoon salt
½ cup (120 milliliters) peanut oil
1 tablespoon Maggi Sauce or daddawa
1 teaspoon curry powder

For Layers:

1 small onion, chopped
½ green pepper, chopped
3 hardboiled eggs, peeled and sliced
½ pound (250 grams) shrimp, cooked and peeled
1 cup cooked, diced meat such as chicken, ham, sausage or corned beef

1. Soak black-eyed peas overnight. Drain. Remove skins (see Skinning black-eyed peas on page 24). This can be done a day or two ahead of time.
2. Combine peas, onion, tomato paste, red pepper and salt in a food processor or blender and process until completely smooth. Add 4 to 6 tablespoons of water if necessary. You should not feel any lumps when you rub mixture between your fingers.
3. Stir oil, Maggi Sauce and curry powder into pea mixture.
4. Combine chopped onions and green peppers in a small bowl.
5. Grease a 9-inch loaf pan. Pour 1½ cup of pea purée in bottom of pan. Layer with half of shrimp and half of onion and pepper mixture.
6. Spread 1 more cup of pea purée in pan. Layer hardboiled egg slices over this. Spread chopped meat on top of egg slices.
7. Spread 1 more cup of purée over meat. Add the remaining shrimp, and then the remaining onion and pepper mixture. Spread the rest of the purée on top.
8. Cover with foil and bake 1 hour at 375ºF (175ºC). Remove foil and bake an additional 15 minutes until the top is browned. Cool in pan 20 minutes before turning out onto rack.

Yield: one 9-inch loaf

Fancy terrine of black-eyed peas

Nigerian women with mortars and pestles, pounding locust beans

Gari Biscuits

Gari (pronounced gah-ree) is a fermented cassava flour which gives these drop biscuits a tantalizing sweet and tangy flavour.

1 cup (140 grams) gari
1 cup (140 grams) all purpose white flour
4 tablespoons butter (½ stick)
1 teaspoon baking powder
½ cup (100 grams) sugar
½ teaspoon salt
1 egg
½ cup (120 milliliters) milk

1. Preheat oven to 400°F (200°C).
2. Sprinkle ½ cup (120 milliliters) of water over gari in a medium bowl. Combine well, breaking up lumps with your hands.
3. Measure flour into medium bowl. Cut butter into flour with a pastry blender until it is the size of small peas.
4. Add baking powder, sugar, salt and gari to the flour mixture.
5. Make a well in the center of flour mixture and pour egg and milk into the well. Stir wet ingredients with a fork to combine, then slowly mix with dry ingredients, until they form a stiff batter.
6. Drop batter by large tablespoonfuls onto a greased cookie sheet. Bake 20 minutes, or until tops are just beginning to turn brown. Remove from pan and cool on a rack.

Yield: 15 biscuits

Note: You can purchase gari at most African food stores.

Paw-Paw Bread

This fragrant quickbread has a very pleasant texture and taste. In our house a loaf disappears almost instantly. You can easily double this recipe and make two loaves. A large, fresh papaya will yield two cups of purée.

1 large papaya (or 1 cup papaya purée)
4 tablespoons butter (½ stick)
¾ cup (150 grams) sugar
2 eggs
1¼ cups (175 grams) white flour
⅛ teaspoon allspice
¾ teaspoon cinnamon
¾ teaspoon salt
¾ teaspoon baking soda
¼ cup raisins (optional)
¼ cup chopped nuts (optional)

1. Preheat oven to 350°F (175°C). Grease a 9-inch loaf or cake pan.
2. Slice papaya lengthwise down the middle and remove the seeds from the center with a large spoon. Peel with a sharp knife, cut remaining fruit into chunks, and purée in a blender or food processor. Reserve one cup of purée, saving the rest for another use.
3. Beat butter and sugar in a mixing bowl until fluffy.
4. Beat eggs into butter mixture one at a time.
5. Stir in papaya purée.
6. Add flour, allspice, cinnamon, salt and baking soda. Mix well.
7. Stir in raisins and nuts if you are using them.
8. Pour batter into prepared pan. Bake in preheated oven for 1 hour, or until knife inserted in center comes out clean. Cool in pan five minutes, then loosen edges with a knife and turn out onto a rack to finish cooling.

Yield: 1 (9-inch) loaf or cake pan

Banana-Rice Bread

In a country where wheat is not commonly grown, West Africans prepare rice bread in many different ways. This Liberian version, baked in either a loaf pan or a round cake pan, is especially light and delicious.

1½ cups (270 grams) rice flour or Cream of Rice cereal
¼ cup (50 grams) sugar
1 tablespoon baking powder
½ teaspoon salt
¼ cup currants or raisins
2 eggs
¾ cup (180 milliliters) milk
2 ripe bananas, mashed
½ cup (120 milliliters) vegetable oil

1. Preheat oven to 325°F (165°C). Grease a 9-inch loaf or cake pan.
2. Mix rice flour, sugar, baking powder, salt and raisins in a large bowl.
3. Whisk together eggs, milk, mashed bananas, and oil in a separate bowl.
4. Add liquid ingredients to dry ingredients, mixing batter thoroughly. Pour batter into the prepared loaf or cake pan.
5. Bake in preheated oven for 50 minutes, or until a knife inserted in middle of pan comes out clean. Cool in pan 5 minutes, then remove from pan and finish cooling on wire rack.

Yield: One (9-inch) loaf or round cake

Note: Rice flour is available in health food stores or through mail order (see Sources).

Banana rice bread

Grilled plantain with red pepper

Grilled Plantain with Red Pepper

In Nigeria, this sweet and spicy snack is called dodo. Be sure to use ripe plantains that are completely yellow with black spots – the green ones do not have enough sugar and will taste dry. As always, you can adjust the seasoning to make them scorching or mild.

Ripe plantains (one per person)
salt and ground red pepper to sprinkle

1. Peel plantains by cutting lengthwise through the peel from top to bottom, then sliding fingers under the peel to pull it off. Cut plantains in half lengthwise to make two long slices, as you would for a banana split. Cut each long slice crosswise in the middle to make four pieces.
2. Sprinkle plantains with salt and red pepper, depending on your taste. Grill until tops are golden brown.

Yield: 1 serving per plantain

Variation: **Fried Plantain with Red Pepper** – Prepare plantains as above in step 1. Sprinkle plantains with red pepper according to taste. Heat 1 cup (240 milliliters) peanut oil in a large skillet. Fry plantains until golden, turning once. Remove from skillet with a slotted spoon and drain on paper towels. Sprinkle with salt before serving.

Note: See photo on page 49.

Smoky Avocado

A creamy avocado heaped with zesty smoked fish filling makes a grand hors d'oeuvre. This unique combination is guaranteed to delight your dinner guests. You can also serve it for a light, exotic lunch.

4 eggs, hardboiled and peeled
¼ cup (60 milliliters) mayonnaise
¼ cup (60 milliliters) lime juice
¼ teaspoon sugar
½ teaspoon salt
⅓ cup (75 milliliters) olive oil
1 small jar pimento or roasted red pepper
½ pound (250 grams) smoked trout, salmon or whitefish, skin and bones removed
2 large, ripe avocados

1. Separate egg yolks from whites. Chop whites finely in a small bowl and set aside.
2. Mash yolks in a deep bowl and stir in mayonnaise. Add lime juice, sugar and salt.
3. Add olive oil to yolk mixture one tablespoon at a time, whisking vigorously. Continue until all of olive oil is combined. Or, you can pour yolk mixture into bowl of food processor and add oil slowly through feed tube while processor is running. Oil should be completely absorbed.
4. Chop pimento or roasted pepper coarsely.
5. Flake fish with a fork into a medium bowl. Add egg whites, pimento and yolk mixture to fish and mix gently.
6. Cut avocados in half lengthwise and remove each seed by plunging the tip of a sharp knife into it and lifting it out, taking care not to mutilate the fruit. Distribute fish mixture evenly and mound on each avocado half. Serve immediately.

Yield: 4 servings

Beef Tsire Grilled in a Spicy Peanut Marinade

In Nigeria these marinated beef strips (pronounced seer-ay) are threaded on skewers, grilled over open air fires and sold in the marketplace. Who could resist this aroma of grilled beef and spices! You can adjust the seasonings to make them mild or scorchingly hot. They make a delicious main course served with rice, or an exotic appetizer. Be sure to leave at least 2 hours to marinate meat before grilling.

> **1 pound (500 grams) top round or sirloin steak, a long, thick cut**
> **½ cup (125 grams) smooth, unsweetened peanut butter**
> **½ teaspoon ground red pepper, or to taste**
> **½ teaspoon salt**
> **½ teaspoon ground powdered ginger**
> **2 tablespoons peanut oil**
> **1 tablespoon lime juice**

1. Slice steak against the grain into strips about ¼-inch (½ centimeter) wide and as long as possible.
2. In a shallow glass pan, mix peanut butter, red pepper, salt, ginger, peanut oil and lime juice until it forms a smooth paste. Rub each meat strip with marinade until thoroughly coated. Use your hands for this – it is messy, but by far the easiest way. Return meat to the glass pan, cover and refrigerate several hours.
3. Soak wooden or bamboo skewers in cold water for at least one hour before using.
4. Thread meat on skewers accordion-style. Do not bunch the meat strips – leave them stretched long on the skewer.
5. Grill or broil strips 15 to 20 minutes until meat is cooked through and coating bubbles. Turn once during cooking.

Yield: About 10 tsire

Note: You can substitute 1½ teaspoons yaji (page 187) for the ginger, red pepper and salt.

Beef tsire grilled in a spicy peanut marinade

Nigerian man cooking tsire in marketplace

photo by Thadd Jackson

Mushrooms on Fried Yam Chips

Earthy mushrooms with a light lemon flavour are a perfect topping for fried yam chips. If yams are not available try them on toast.

> 1 pound (500 grams) small white mushrooms
> 2 tablespoons butter
> 2 tablespoons peanut oil
> 4 scallions, chopped
> ¼ sweet green pepper, seeded and chopped
> 1 hot green or red pepper, seeded and chopped
> ½ teaspoon salt
> 2 tablespoons lemon juice
> fried yam chips (recipe follows)

1. Wash mushrooms. Slice only the large ones. Keep the smaller ones whole.
2. Heat butter and oil in large skillet and sauté mushrooms until water has evaporated and they are lightly browned. Remove from pan and keep warm.
3. Add scallions and sweet and hot peppers to skillet. Saute until soft, about 10 minutes.
4. Return mushrooms to skillet. Add salt and lemon juice. Serve on yam slices or toast.

Yield: 2 servings as a meal; 4 as an appetizer

Fried Yam Chips

> 1 large or two small yams, totaling about 2 pounds (1 kilogram)
> 1 cup (240 milliliters) oil for frying

1. Peel yam and slice in ¼-inch slices.
2. Heat oil in large, heavy skillet. When a tiny piece of yam dropped in the oil begins to sizzle, you are ready to fry.
3. Fry yam slices in oil until just beginning to turn yellow on both sides, about 10 minutes. They should still be soft and not crispy when you take them from the oil. Some yams will develop a bitter taste if you fry them too long. Drain on towels and serve hot.

Yield: About 30 yam chips

Eggplant-Peanut Butter Spread

You can spread this thick and fragrant mixture on fried yam chips (recipe on opposite page) or use it as a dip for fresh vegetables.

1 small tomato
1 small eggplant, about 1 pound (500 grams)
¼ cup (60 milliliters) peanut oil
1 tablespoon smooth, unsweetened peanut butter
½ teaspoon salt

1. Peel tomato by dropping in boiling water for 1 minute, then running under cold water. Skin should slip off easily.
2. Cut tomato in quarters and scoop out seeds with the tip of a sharp knife. Discard seeds.
3. Peel eggplant and cut in slices about ¼ inch (½ centimeter) thick. Heat 2 tablespoons of the oil in a large skillet and fry half of the eggplant slices until very soft and golden brown on both sides. Fry second batch using remaining 2 tablespoons of oil. If necessary, add one or two tablespoons of oil during frying.
4. Meanwhile, mix peanut butter, chopped tomato and salt in a medium bowl. Add eggplant slices to this mixture as they are done, and pound mixture with a pestle or heavy spoon. Continue to pound until all of eggplant is smoothly mixed with the ingredients.
5. Let spread sit at room temperature for 30 minutes before serving.

Yield: 2 cups

Eggplant peanut butter spread with fried yam chips

Spicy Ginger Dipping Sauce

This fiery sauce is a perfect dip for many fried snacks or appetizers.

1 tomato
1 onion
4 cloves garlic
2 fresh hot peppers, seeded if desired
1 inch (2½ centimeter) piece fresh ginger, peeled
1 tablespoon tomato paste
1 tablespoon ground crayfish (optional)
¼ teaspoon ground red pepper
½ teaspoon salt
2 tablespoons peanut oil

1. Peel tomato by dropping in boiling water for 1 minute, then running under cold water. Skin should slip off easily. Cut tomato in quarters and scoop out seeds with the tip of a sharp knife. Discard seeds.
2. Chop tomato, onion, garlic, peppers and ginger into several large pieces each, and combine in food processor or blender. Purée until smooth.
3. Add tomato paste, dried crayfish, ground red pepper and salt to mixture.
4. Heat oil in medium skillet. Add puréed vegetables with 1 cup (240 milliliters) water. Simmer, uncovered, about 20 minutes.

Yield: 1 cup

Creamy Peanut Sauce

This mild, nutty sauce is a delicious dip for steamed vegetables or topping for rice.

1 tablespoon butter
1 tablespoon flour
¼ cup (60 grams) smooth, unsweetened peanut butter
1½ cups (360 milliliters) broth
¼ teaspoon salt
¼ teaspoon sugar

1. Melt butter in skillet. Add flour and stir until smooth. Continue to cook and stir for 1 minute on medium heat until slightly browned.
2. Add peanut butter and stir until blended. Add broth and stir until smooth.
3. Add salt and sugar. Simmer over medium heat, uncovered, until thick, about 10 minutes.

Yield: 1½ cups

Spicy Peanut Sauce

Try this spicier peanut sauce or dip with steamed vegetables, shrimp or rice. Using tomato paste will make your sauce smoother. If you like a chunky dip, go with the fresh tomato.

1 tablespoon peanut oil
1 onion, chopped
1 tomato, chopped, or 1 tablespoon tomato paste
½ green pepper, seeded and chopped
½ teaspoon salt
¼ teaspoon ground red pepper
2 tablespoons smooth, unsweetened peanut butter
1 cup (240 milliliters) broth

1. Heat oil in a medium-sized skillet. Add the onion. Simmer over medium heat until soft, about 5 minutes.
2. Add tomato (or tomato paste), green pepper, salt and red pepper. Continue to simmer another 10 minutes.
3. In a small bowl, mix peanut butter with broth until smooth. Stir into vegetable mixture. Simmer over medium heat until thick, about 10 minutes.

Yield: 2 cups

Soups

Curried cream soup with black-eyed peas

S picy and filling, these soups make excellent appetizers served in small portions as a prelude to an exotic meal. West Africans will often refer to sauces as soup, as in palm nut soup or pepper soup. These recipes are served as a sauce with rice or fufu, and can be found in the miya section.

Contents

Chicken soup with yam and hot pepper garnished with koro-koro

Chicken Soup with Yam and Hot Pepper

This spicy chicken soup, also called Blessing Soup, is a festival dish served after the harvest in West Africa.

1 whole chicken, skinned and cut in 3 to 4 large pieces
1 onion, chopped
1 fresh hot green or red pepper, chopped
1 teaspoon salt
½ teaspoon ground red pepper, or to taste
2 tablespoons peanut oil
2 tablespoons chopped fresh parsley
1 large or several small yams, total weight about 1½ pounds (750 grams)

1. Pour 8 cups (2 liters) water over chicken pieces in a large pot and bring to a boil. Simmer uncovered over medium-high heat for about 15 minutes, until chicken is partially cooked.
2. Add onion, fresh peppers, salt, ground red pepper, oil and parsley. Continue to simmer 10 minutes.
3. Remove chicken pieces from pot and leave until cool enough to handle. Pull meat from bones and break into small pieces. Return chicken meat to pot and discard bones.
4. Peel yams and cut into ½-inch cubes. Add yams to pot and continue to simmer, uncovered, another 10 to 15 minutes, until yams are tender.

Yield: 6 servings

Coconut Milk

Coconut milk is used frequently in West African cooking, especially in the coastal areas. You can buy canned coconut milk and save yourself a lot of time in preparation. However if you want to make your own from scratch, begin with a fresh coconut. Make sure that you can hear liquid sloshing inside when you shake it, and that it is not moldy. The first step is to crack the coconut and grate the meat. Then you will pour hot water over the grated meat to extract the oil, and this rich white liquid is the milk.

How to Crack and Grate a Coconut

1. Preheat oven to 400°F (200°C).
2. Locate the 3 "eyes" at the top of the coconut, and pierce the soft one with a metal skewer. Drain the water, shaking the coconut to get all of it out. You can either discard this water or save it for another use.
3. Place the whole coconut on the oven rack and bake 15 minutes.
4. Remove the coconut from the oven and if the shell is not already broken give it a good whack with a hammer across the middle. It should crack easily. When the coconut is cool enough to handle, pry the shell off the brown flesh inside. If you can do this without breaking the coconut into pieces it will be easier to peel.
5. Under the shell the coconut is covered with a thin brown membrane. Peel this away with a sharp paring knife, revealing the white flesh underneath. Be careful with this – always point the knife away from your hands while you are cutting.
6. Grate the coconut flesh in a food processor or by hand.

Yield: 4 to 5 cups (14 ounces/400 grams) loosely packed grated coconut

Making Coconut Milk

1. Pour 2 cups boiling water over the grated meat from one coconut. Leave at room temperature 20 minutes.
2. Strain the liquid from the pulp, squeezing and pressing to extract as much liquid as possible. Discard the grated coconut.

Yield: 2 cups (475 milliliters) coconut milk

Coconut Soup

A small serving of this clear, shimmering broth is packed with rich and spicy flavour, setting the stage for an exotic meal. If you are short on time and do not want to crack a coconut, dried unsweetened coconut will work fine. On the other hand, grating a fresh coconut will leave you with some extra to use in other recipes or for a garnish.

3½ cups (850 milliliters) broth
1½ cups (150 grams) fresh grated coconut, or ¾ cup (75 grams) dried unsweetened grated coconut
1 small eggplant, about ½ pound (250 grams), peeled and diced
1 tablespoon lemon juice
½ teaspoon salt
¼ teaspoon ground ginger
2 tablespoons chopped fresh parsley

1. To shell and grate fresh coconut follow the instructions on preceding page.
2. Combine broth and coconut in large saucepan and bring to a boil over medium-high heat.
3. Add eggplant and lemon juice. Cover, lower heat and simmer 35 minutes.
4. Press mixture through a sieve or food mill, and return liquid to the saucepan. Discard solid scraps.
5. Add salt and ginger. Bring to a simmer again, then remove from heat and serve immediately. Sprinkle parsley over individual portions and garnish with fresh grated coconut if you have it on hand.

Yield: 4 (¾ cup) servings

Curried Cream Soup with Black-eyed Peas

If you use canned coconut milk and beans, this rich, creamy soup takes very little time to prepare. A small serving is just enough to whet the appetite as the first course for a West African meal.

½ cup (120 grams) canned black-eyed peas
2 cups (475 milliliters) or 1 can coconut milk
1 onion, sliced thin
2 tomatoes, sliced thin
¼ teaspoon ground red pepper
1 teaspoon curry powder
¼ teaspoon salt

1. Drain peas and combine with coconut milk in a medium saucepan. Simmer gently over medium-low heat until peas are heated through.
2. Add onion, tomatoes, red pepper, curry powder and salt. Bring to a slow boil and simmer, partially covered, 30 minutes. If soup gets too thick add a small amount of water. Serve warm.

Yield: 2 large (1½ cup) or 4 small (¾ cup) servings

Note: See photo on page 59.

Spicy Cream of Spinach Soup

This soup is delicious with spinach, but you can choose from just about any type of fresh dark, leafy greens including mustard, turnip, beet, dandelions or collards.

2 tablespoons peanut oil
1 onion, chopped
1 pound (500 grams) fresh spinach or other greens, washed, stemmed and chopped (8 cups)
2 cups (475 milliliters) broth
½ teaspoon salt
¼ teaspoon ground red pepper, or to taste
½ cup (120 milliliters) light cream or half and half

1. Heat oil in a large, heavy or non-stick pot. Add onion and simmer 5 minutes.
2. Add the greens and broth. Cover and simmer over low heat 45 minutes, or until greens are very tender.
3. Allow mixture to cool slightly and purée in a blender or food processor. You may need to do this in batches. You can also press through a sieve.
4. Return mixture to soup pan, and add salt and red pepper.
5. Stir in cream just before serving and keep on low heat until heated through.

Yield: 2 large (1½ cup) or 4 small (¾ cup) servings

Note: You can substitute a 10-ounce package (300 grams) frozen spinach or 2 cups cooked spinach for the fresh spinach.

Ancient Empires: Songhai

The city of Gao, which began to form around 500 A.D., grew strong enough to overthrow Mali and establish the Songhai empire in the 15th century. Sunni Ali Ber of Gao took control of Timbuktu in 1468, driving the Mossi people south. His armies patrolled the waters of the Niger River, keeping a firm watch on traders from their fleet of canoes. Commerce grew under the security of this system. However, universities such as Sankore declined during Ali Ber's rule since Muslim scholars were not attracted to his land. He favored traditional religions. In fact, he himself was said to be a formidable magician. According to stories he could turn himself into a vulture and make his army invisible. Sunni Ali Ber died in a drowning accident in 1492.

Askia Mohammed, the next to come to power, was a devout Muslim, and the University of Sankore in Timbuktu began to grow again. Askia Mohammed turned Songhai into the largest empire in the history of West Africa.

Once again in the 16th century, relentless raids from the desert Berbers weakened the empire. Songhai tried to move east into Hausaland, and was beaten back. The Europeans were on the coast by now, and trans-Saharan trade was beginning to dry up. Slave traders were coming further inland, and raiding Songhai to meet their demand. The last and largest West African empire began to decline. In the end it was a small army of Moroccans who overpowered the Songhai with firearms. After defeating the Songhai, Morocco did not have enough strength to maintain the empire, and it disintegrated. Today the Songhai descendants live mostly in Mali and Niger.

Aiki yaro inda ya so ka fi ganin hanzarinasa.
Send a boy where he wants to go and you will see his best pace.

Rice Entrées and Side Dishes

Seafood coconut rice with tomatoes

Rice is grown in many of the wet coastal and river areas of West Africa. A rice dish containing several different meats and vegetables can be a meal by itself. In Hausa, a dish of rice with many different meat and vegetable ingredients is called *dafa duka,* which means *cook everything. Jollof rice* is another delicious dish served almost throughout West Africa. It can be made with any type of meat or vegetable, but is always red with tomato paste. Creamy *coconut rice* is more regional, prepared in southern coastal areas where the coconut palm grows and seafood is plentiful. All of these recipes adapt well to whatever ingredients you have on hand.

Contents

Curried rice with beef

Wahala mudu che in ta chika sai a juye.

Trouble is like a measure, when it is full turn it out.

Check Rice

Dark greens mixed with creamy white rice make this Liberian specialty a colourful side dish. It goes well with a light entrée such as fish in coconut milk, or with tsire. You can experiment with different types of greens. Beet greens add a lovely pink colour to the rice.

1 teaspoon salt
1½ cups (300 grams) long-grain white rice
½ pound (250 grams) fresh spinach, kale or beet greens, stemmed and chopped (4 to 5 cups)

1. Combine 3 cups (725 milliliters) water with the salt in a medium saucepan and bring to a boil. Add rice, lower heat and cover. Simmer 10 minutes.
2. Spread greens over top of rice, cover again and cook on low heat another 5 to 10 minutes, or until rice is soft and water is absorbed. Fold greens into rice before serving.

Yield: 4 servings

Note: You can substitute 5 ounces (150 grams) frozen or 1 cup cooked spinach for the fresh spinach. See photo on page 142.

Rice with Black-eyed Peas

Plenty of peanut oil adds a velvety texture to this spicy twist on rice and beans.

½ cup (100 grams) dried black-eyed peas, soaked overnight, or 1 cup canned black-eyed peas
½ cup (120 milliliters) peanut oil
1 onion, chopped
3 tomatoes, chopped
2 tablespoons tomato paste
½ teaspoon ground red pepper
½ teaspoon salt
1½ cups (300 grams) long-grain white rice
3 cups (725 milliliters) broth

1. Cover black-eyed peas with water in a medium saucepan, bring to a boil and simmer over medium heat until soft, about 1 hour. Drain and set aside. If you are using canned peas, drain and measure 1 cup.
2. Heat oil in large, heavy pot. Add onion, tomatoes, tomato paste, red pepper, and salt. Simmer 10 minutes, uncovered, over medium heat until vegetables are soft.
3. Add rice, and broth to pan. Bring to a boil. Cover, lower heat and cook about 15 minutes until rice is tender. Stir black-eyed peas into rice. Cover and let sit 5 minutes before serving.

Yield: 4 servings

Coconut Rice with Pork

Simmering this rice in coconut milk instead of water makes it rich and creamy. Use a heavy or non-stick pan so the rice does not burn. Canned coconut milk is convenient for this recipe and can be found in most supermarkets. Be sure to get pure coconut milk with no sugar or other additives.

1 tablespoon peanut oil
1 pound (500 grams) pork, cut in small chunks
½ teaspoon salt
3 cups (725 milliliters) unsweetened coconut milk
1½ cups (300 grams) long-grain white rice

1. Heat oil in a large, heavy or nonstick pan. Add pork and salt. Simmer until browned.
2. Add coconut milk and bring to a boil over medium heat. Add rice, lower heat, and cook, covered, about 15 minutes. Add a small amount of water if it begins to stick to the pan. When the rice is done it should be soft and not chewy.
3. Turn off the heat and let the covered rice sit 5 to 10 minutes before serving.

Yield: 4 servings

Variation: **Coconut Rice with Shrimp** – To substitute shrimp for the pork, omit the first step. Begin with boiling the coconut milk, and add shrimp during the last 10 minutes of cooking. You can use precooked or raw, peeled shrimp.

Seafood Coconut Rice with Tomato

The onion, pepper and tomato give this creamy rice an extra dimension of texture and taste. This recipe is mild; if you want a spicy rice, substitute hot peppers for the sweet green pepper. You can add any type of cooked seafood along with the fish and shrimp. Be sure you use pure, unsweetened coconut milk.

1 onion
1 green pepper
1 tomato
2 cups (475 milliliters) unsweetened coconut milk (or 1 can)
½ teaspoon salt
1 cup (200 grams) long-grain white rice
½ pound (250 grams) lean white fish fillets such as haddock, cut in several large pieces
½ pound (250 grams) raw shrimp, peeled

1. Cut onion, green pepper, and tomato in half. Grind one half of each together in food processor or blender until smooth. Slice remaining halves into thin slices.
2. Heat coconut milk, ground vegetables and salt in a large, heavy or nonstick pan over medium heat until boiling. Add rice, cover and simmer on low heat for 10 minutes. Add 1 cup (240 milliliters) water, cover and continue to simmer until rice is tender, about 10 minutes.
3. Add sliced vegetables, fish and shrimp to the rice, and stir gently. Cover and cook 10 minutes more, until the vegetables are tender and the seafood is cooked through. Serve immediately.

Yield: 4 servings

Note: See photo on page 67.

Curried Rice with Beef

This dish is a good example of the Hausa dafa duka, or "cook everything." A cook might add any combination of meats or vegetables on hand that day.

3 tablespoons peanut oil or palm oil
½ pound (250 grams) beef, cut in chunks
1 tomato, chopped
2 tablespoons tomato paste
1 onion, chopped
½ teaspoon curry powder
½ teaspoon salt
½ teaspoon ground red pepper
1 cup (200 grams) long-grain white rice

1. Heat oil in a large, heavy or nonstick pan and simmer beef over medium heat until browned, about 10 minutes.
2. Add tomato, tomato paste, onion, curry powder, salt, and red pepper. Continue to simmer 10 minutes, until vegetables are soft.
3. Add rice and 2 cups (475 milliliters) water. Stir well, lower heat and simmer, covered, 15 to 20 minutes, until rice is soft and water is absorbed. Check during cooking and add more water if necessary.

Yield: 4 servings

Note: See photo on page 69.

Curried Rice with Tomato and Greens

Substituting dark, leafy greens for the meat makes this recipe a lighter and more colourful side dish. It can also be served as a main course with a salad and bread.

¼ cup (60 milliliters) peanut oil
1 onion, chopped
½ teaspoon salt
½ teaspoon curry powder
¼ teaspoon ground red pepper
1 tomato, chopped
3 tablespoons tomato paste
1½ cups (300 grams) long-grain white rice
¼ pound (125 grams) fresh dark, leafy greens such as kale or spinach, stemmed and chopped (2 to 3 cups)

1. Heat oil in a large, heavy or nonstick pan over medium heat. Add onion and simmer, uncovered, about 5 minutes, until translucent.
2. Add salt, curry powder, and red pepper. Continue to simmer 5 minutes more.
3. Add tomato and tomato paste. Continue to simmer about 10 minutes.
4. Add rice, and continue to cook uncovered over medium heat until kernels begin to turn white, about 5 minutes.
5. Add 3 cups (725 milliliters) of water and bring to a boil. Lower heat, cover and simmer about 15 minutes, until rice is tender and water is absorbed.
6. Add chopped greens, cover, and simmer 5 minutes more over low heat until greens are wilted.

Yield: 4 servings

Note: You can substitute 3 to 4 ounces (125 grams) frozen or 1 cup cooked greens for fresh greens.

Jollof Rice with Chicken, Beef and Ham

Jollof rice is always bright red with tomato paste. Combining meats is common in West African cooking. The decadent blend of three different meats in this dish gives it very rich flavour.

3 tablespoons peanut oil
½ pound (250 grams) beef, cut in chunks
2 pounds (1 kilogram) chicken pieces
2 onions, chopped
2 tomatoes, chopped
¼ cup (100 grams) tomato paste
2 cloves garlic
2 fresh hot peppers, chopped, or ½ teaspoon ground red pepper
½ teaspoon ground ginger
1 teaspoon salt
1 bay leaf
3 cups (725 milliliters) broth
½ pound (250 grams) ham, cut in chunks
1½ cups (300 grams) long-grain white rice
3 hardboiled eggs, peeled and sliced

1. Heat oil in a large, heavy or non-stick pan over medium-high heat and brown beef and chicken on all sides. Remove from pan and keep warm.
2. Add onions to pan, lower heat to medium, and cook until soft, about 5 minutes.
3. Add tomatoes, tomato paste, garlic, peppers, ginger, salt and bay leaf. Continue to simmer 10 minutes, uncovered.
4. Add broth and ham, bring to a boil and simmer another 10 minutes, uncovered.
5. Add chicken pieces, beef and rice. Cover, lower heat and simmer about 20 minutes, until chicken is cooked through and rice is soft.
6. Remove from heat and let sit 5 to 10 minutes before serving. Garnish with hardboiled eggs.

Yield: 6 large servings

Note: You can substitute 1½ teaspoons yaji (page 187) and ½ teaspoon salt for the ginger, red pepper and salt.

Jollof Rice with Vegetables

This is a velvety vegetarian version of the classic rosy red jollof rice. The combination of spices gives it a hot edge without being overpowering. If you really like your food fiery you can increase the red pepper. It has just enough palm oil to give it an exotic taste. If they do not know West African foods, your friends will never guess the secret ingredient!

1 small eggplant
½ small cabbage
6 tablespoons peanut oil
1 tablespoon palm oil (or 1 extra tablespoon peanut oil)
1 onion, chopped
2 tomatoes, chopped
2 green peppers, chopped
1½ cups (300 grams) long-grain white rice
3 cups (725 milliliters) broth
2 tablespoons tomato paste
⅛ teaspoon black pepper
¼ teaspoon ground ginger
¼ teaspoon ground red pepper
1 teaspoon salt
2 teaspoons brown sugar
¼ teaspoon thyme

1. Prepare cabbage and eggplant first: peel eggplant, cut into ¾-inch chunks, and fry in 3 tablespoons of oil until golden; slice cabbage leaves into long, wide strips and steam until just soft, about 5 minutes, and drain. Keep cabbage and eggplant warm in a covered saucepan.
2. Heat remaining 3 tablespoons peanut and the palm oil over medium heat in large, heavy or non-stick pot. Add onion, tomatoes and green peppers and simmer until vegetables are soft, about 10 minutes.
3. Add rice, broth, tomato paste, black pepper, ginger, red pepper, salt, brown sugar and thyme. Bring to a boil, cover and lower heat. Simmer until rice is cooked, about 15 to 20 minutes. Remove from heat, stir, then replace cover and let rice set for 5 minutes.
4. Add eggplant and cabbage to pot. Stir gently to mix, and serve.

Yield: 6 large servings

Note: You can substitute 1 teaspoon yaji (page 187) and ½ tsp salt for the ginger, red pepper and salt. See photo on page 79.

Senegal Fish and Rice

This dish is known as tiebou dienne (chay-bou-jen) and is considered the national dish of Senegal. As with most West African dishes, it comes in many variations but always includes rice, fish, and several vegetables.

½ pound (250 grams) eggplant
2 tablespoons peanut oil
¼ small head of cabbage
1 cup (200 grams) long-grain white rice
3 tablespoons tomato paste
2 carrots, peeled and sliced in rings
2 fresh hot peppers, seeded and chopped (more if desired)
½ pound (250 grams) whole okra, stem ends removed
1 onion, coarsely chopped
1 green pepper, coarsely chopped
2 tablespoons peanut oil
¾ teaspoon salt
1½ pounds (750 grams) lean, white fish, filleted and cut in 6 large pieces

1. Peel eggplant and cut into ½-inch (1½ centimeter) cubes. Heat 2 tablespoons peanut oil in heavy skillet and cook eggplant until browned and soft. Set aside, covered.
2. Bring 4 cups (1 liter) of water to a boil in a saucepan, add cabbage and boil 10 minutes, covered. Drain and cut into thin strips. Set aside with eggplant.
3. Bring 2 cups (475 milliliters) of water to a boil in a large, heavy or non-stick pot. Add rice, tomato paste, carrots, peppers and okra. Lower heat, cover and simmer 15 minutes until rice is tender. Remove from heat and let stand while fish is prepared.
4. While rice is cooking, grind onion and green pepper in food processor or blender until smooth.
5. Heat 2 tablespoons peanut oil in a large skillet. Add ground vegetables and salt and simmer 10 minutes. Add fish fillets, cover and simmer 10 minutes, or until fish is opaque and begins to flake.
6. Stir eggplant and cabbage into rice. Serve rice with fish and sauce.

Yield: 6 servings

Senegal fish and rice

Jollof rice with cabbage and other vegetables

Ancient Empires: Kanem-Bornu

According to local legend the So, who lived around Lake Chad thousands of years ago, were a race of giants. They stood 20 elbows tall, and one man could kill an elephant and carry it home on his shoulders. While this may be an elaboration, archaeologists have found huge pottery vessels made by the So, probably used as burial urns.

Berber nomads began to drift down from the desert and settle in this area, either mingling with or conquering the So people. The descendants of the Berbers were the Kanuri, founders of Kanem State.

By the 11th century Kanem was growing rich from the Saharan trade. They controlled the valuable salt mines of Bilma; salt was traded ounce for ounce with gold in Ghana to the west. Slaves were also a hot commodity in North Africa, and Kanem raided the people to their south to meet this demand.

After about 200 years the center of power shifted to the west. The Kanuri people in Bornu took over most of the Kanem empire. The Bornu empire stretched into Nigeria. The Hausa city of Kano was paying tribute to Bornu until the Fulanis took control. The ruler, or mai, who brought Bornu to full power was Idris Alooma. His army rode camels, and with this mobility they managed to drive the Tuaregs out of their northern territory. Idris Alooma also used firearms against his enemies, who still fought only with swords and bows. Bornu flourished right up until the time of colonialism, in the 19th century.

Zumunta a kafa ta ke.
Relationship is in the foot.

Vegetables on the Side

Yam with red pepper and greens

The yam is a staple of many West African societies, and can be prepared in countless ways. Many varieties of yams and other root vegetables are available in supermarkets even in colder climates. Name *(pronounced nah-may)* is the most similar to African yams. Some Spanish markets carry frozen name, already peeled and cut in chunks. This is a wonderful convenience food, perfect for modern West African cooks. If you can not find any type of yams, you can substitute potatoes in these recipes. Side dishes of cassava, beans, plantains, mangos, pumpkin, tomato relish and okra are also included here.

Contents

photo by Thadd Jackson

Hausa woman with bowl of cassava

Fresh yam from Ghana, about 10 inches long

Gari

Plantain Salad Imoyo

Plantains take the place of potatoes or pasta in this robust salad with a tropical twist.

2 ripe plantains (completely yellow with black spots)
¼ cup (60 milliliters) olive oil
2 tablespoons lime juice
½ teaspoon salt
¼ teaspoon black pepper
½ green bell pepper, seeded and sliced in long, thin slices
1 fresh red hot pepper, seeded and chopped
1 small cucumber, peeled, seeded and diced into ¼ inch cubes

1. Peel plantains. This will be easier if you cut through the peel lengthwise and slide your fingers under the skin to pull it off. Place whole plantains in a medium saucepan and cover with water. Bring to a boil, then simmer 10 minutes until the plantains are tender enough to pierce with a fork. (Green plantains will take longer to cook) Drain plantains and set aside to cool.
2. Whisk oil, lime juice, salt and pepper together in a small bowl until they become creamy, about 5 minutes.
3. Combine bell pepper, hot pepper and cucumber in a large bowl.
4. Slice cooled plantains on a diagonal into ½-inch (1½ centimeter) slices. Add to bowl of vegetables.
5. Pour marinade over vegetables and mix well. Serve at room temperature.

Yield: 4 servings

Imoyo dishes combine the sultry and spicy West African foods with Brazilian ingredients and cooking methods. In the 15th century the Portuguese began a thriving slave trade and sent many West Africans to their colonies in Brazil. When slavery was outlawed by the British in the 19th century, some of these slaves regained their freedom, returned to Africa and settled along the coast of Nigeria. They brought with them green peppers, olive oil and garlic, which were not traditionally used in Nigerian cooking. Imoyo dishes often feature vegetables marinated in vinegar, lime or lemon juice.

Plantain salad imoyo

Black-eyed Peas and Plantain in Palm Oil

This recipe is based on awoojoh beans, a festival dish from Sierra Leone. You need red palm oil to get the deep, robust colour and flavour. Plantain adds a balance of sweetness to this spicy side dish. If you are using dried peas be sure to leave time to soak them overnight and boil them for about an hour.

1 cup (200 grams) dried black-eyed peas, soaked overnight, or 2½ cups canned peas
1 ripe plantain
¼ cup (60 milliliters) red palm oil
1 onion, chopped
½ teaspoon salt
½ teaspoon red pepper

1. If you are using dried peas, cover with water in a saucepan and boil until tender, about 1 hour. Drain. If you are using canned peas simply drain them.
2. Peel plantain by cutting with a sharp knife through the peel lengthwise from top to bottom, then sliding fingers under the peel and pulling it off. Slice in ½-inch (1½ centimeter) rounds.
3. Heat palm oil in a large, heavy skillet until melted. Add onion, salt and pepper and fry about 5 minutes, on medium-high heat, until soft. Add peas and plantain slices, and continue to fry for 20 minutes, uncovered, stirring occasionally to brown ingredients well.

Yield: 4 servings

Black-eyed peas and plantain in palm oil

Gari foto

Gari Foto

Tangy gari (pronounced gah-ree) is fermented and toasted cassava meal. This preparation is popular in many West African countries.

½ cup (120 milliliters) broth
1 cup (140 grams) gari
3 tablespoons peanut oil
1 onion, chopped
1 tomato, chopped
1 red bell pepper, seeded and chopped
¼ teaspoon ground red pepper
¼ teaspoon ground ginger
½ teaspoon salt
2 eggs

1. Pour broth over gari in a small bowl. Mix well, breaking up lumps with your hands.
2. Heat oil in a large skillet. Add chopped onion and tomato. Simmer over medium heat, stirring occasionally, until most of liquid has evaporated from vegetables, about 15 minutes.
3. Add chopped red pepper, ground red pepper, ginger and salt. Continue to cook 5 more minutes until red peppers begin to get soft.
4. Add gari to skillet, and cook 5 minutes, stirring, until heated through.
5. Beat eggs together in a small bowl. Add to skillet and cook, stirring, until eggs are set, about 5 minutes. Eggs may also be scrambled separately and served on the side. Serve warm.

Yield: 4 servings

Note: You can substitute 1 teaspoon yaji (page 187) for the ginger, red pepper and salt. Gari is available in most stores which sell African foods. See photos on pages 83 and 87.

Fried Pumpkin

If you have only had pumpkin in a pie, you are in for a treat when you taste this dish. Pumpkin has a deeper flavour than most of its cousins in the squash family. This hearty side dish will add a splash of bright orange to your meal.

½ small (2 pound/1 kilogram) fresh pumpkin or yellow squash
1 teaspoon salt
¼ cup (60 milliliters) peanut oil
salt and pepper for seasoning

1. Remove seeds and stem from pumpkin, and peel skin with a very sharp paring knife. Cut pumpkin into 1-inch (2½ centimeter) cubes.
2. Cover pumpkin with water in a small saucepan, add salt and bring to a boil. Simmer 5 minutes over medium heat, until pumpkin is just barely tender when you poke it with a fork. Keep an eye on this, because if it cooks too long the pumpkin will start to fall apart. Drain pumpkin and set aside.
3. Heat oil in a large skillet, add pumpkin cubes, and fry over medium-high heat, stirring occasionally, about 10 minutes, or until heated through and golden. Season to taste. Serve hot.

Yield: 4 servings

Diced Tomato Salad

This makes a wonderful topping for groundnut chop, or a cool, summery side dish. You can prepare it up to two days ahead and store in the refrigerator. The spicy tomato relish has a refreshing lemon flavour.

2 large, ripe tomatoes
1 tablespoon lemon juice
¼ teaspoon ground red pepper
¼ teaspoon salt

1. Peel tomatoes by dropping in boiling water for 1 minute, then running under cold water. Skins should slip off easily.
2. Cut tomatoes in quarters and scoop out seeds with the tip of a sharp knife. Discard seeds.
3. Dice tomato and combine with lemon juice, red pepper and salt. Let stand at room temperature at least 30 minutes before serving.

Yield: 1½ cups

Cool Okra with Spices

Okra lovers will enjoy the firm yet slippery texture of this dish. Serve as a topping for groundnut chop or a cool side salad. You can make it up to two days ahead and store in the refrigerator.

1 small onion, finely minced
2 cloves garlic, minced
¼ teaspoon ground red pepper
¼ teaspoon black pepper
¼ teaspoon salt
10 ounces (300 grams) okra, fresh or frozen, stemmed and sliced crosswise into 3 pieces

1. Combine 1½ cups (360 milliliters) water, onion, garlic, red pepper, black pepper and salt in a small, heavy saucepan. Bring to a boil.
2. Add okra, bring back to a boil and simmer over low to medium heat 15 minutes. Stir occasionally and be careful not to let it burn.
3. Remove from heat and transfer to serving bowl with a slotted spoon, draining off and discarding any remaining liquid. Serve at room temperature or refrigerate until cool.

Yield: 1½ cup

Yam with Greens, Onion and Okra

This dish makes me think of parsley potatoes, African style. You can use any type of dark, leafy greens such as spinach, kale, or turnip greens.

1 large or 2 small yams, totaling about 1½ pounds (750 grams)
¼ cup (60 milliliters) peanut oil
1 onion, chopped
¼ pound (125 grams) fresh spinach or kale, stemmed and chopped (2 to 3 cups)
¼ pound (125 grams) fresh or frozen okra, stemmed and sliced in thin slices crosswise
½ teaspoon salt
1 to 2 fresh hot peppers, seeded and minced

1. Peel yams and cut into 1-inch (2½ centimeter) cubes.
2. Cover yams with water in a medium sized saucepan and bring to a boil. Boil 5 minutes, until just barely tender. Drain and set aside.
3. Heat oil in a large skillet. Add onion and cook 5 minutes over medium heat. Add chopped greens, okra, salt and peppers. Continue to simmer about 20 minutes, until vegetables are soft.
4. Stir yams into skillet mixture. Serve warm.

Yield: 4 servings

Note: You can substitute 3 to 4 ounces (125 grams) frozen or 1 cup cooked greens for the fresh greens.

Yam with Green Beans

Long, curly green beans are common in West Africa. Leave your beans whole with just the ends trimmed.

> **1 large or 2 small yams, totaling about 1½ pounds (750 grams)**
> **½ pound (250 grams) green beans, ends trimmed (2 cups)**
> **½ cup (120 milliliters) peanut oil**
> **1 onion, chopped**
> **½ teaspoon ground red pepper**
> **1 tomato, sliced**
> **½ teaspoon salt**

1. Peel yams with a sharp paring knife, and cut into 1-inch (2½ centimeter) cubes.
2. Place green beans in a large pot and cover with water. Bring to a boil and simmer, covered, 10 minutes. Add yams and simmer until soft when pierced with a fork, 5 to10 minutes. Drain vegetables, return to pot and cover.
3. Heat oil in a large skillet. Add onion and simmer 5 minutes over medium heat. Add red pepper, tomato and salt, and continue to cook another 10 minutes, stirring.
4. Add onion mixture to the beans and yams. Mix well and serve hot.

Yield: 4 servings

Yam with Green Peas

The generous oil and tomato paste gives these yams a golden glow. You can use less oil if you prefer. The dish will not be as radiant, but it will still taste delicious.

> 1 large or several small yams, totaling about 1½ pounds (750 grams)
> ¾ pound (375 grams) fresh green peas (1½ cups/10 ounce package frozen)
> ½ cup (120 milliliters) peanut oil
> 1 onion, sliced
> 1 tablespoon tomato paste
> ½ teaspoon salt
> ¼ teaspoon red pepper

1. Peel yam and cut into 1-inch (2½ centimeter) cubes. Cover with water in a medium saucepan, add peas, and bring to a boil. Simmer over medium heat until yam is just tender enough to be pierced with a fork, 5 to 10 minutes. Drain and set aside.
2. Heat oil in a large skillet. Add onion, tomato paste, salt and red pepper and cook over medium-high heat until onion is soft, about 5 minutes.
3. In a large serving bowl, combine yam mixture with onion. Mix well and serve warm.

Yield: 4 servings

Yam with Red Peppers and Greens

Colourful tints of red and green will liven up your table as you serve this savory vegetable dish.

1 large or several small yams, totaling 1½ pounds (750 grams)
¼ cup (60 milliliters) peanut oil
1 onion, thinly sliced
½ pound (250 grams) kale or other dark, leafy greens, stemmed and chopped (4 cups)
3 fresh red peppers, seeded and chopped
¼ pound (125 grams) fresh or frozen okra, stemmed and sliced thinly (¾ cup)
½ teaspoon salt

1. Peel yams and cut into 1-inch (2½ centimeter) cubes. Cover with water in small saucepan and bring to a boil. Simmer 5 to 10 minutes, or until just tender enough to pierce with a fork. Drain and set aside.
2. Heat oil in large skillet. Add sliced onion and cook over medium heat 5 minutes, until soft.
3. Add chopped greens, red peppers, okra and salt to skillet. Continue to cook, stirring occasionally, for 10 minutes.
4. Add yams and cook, stirring frequently, until heated through.

Yield: 4 servings

Note: You can substitute 6 ounces (175 grams) frozen or 2 cups cooked kale or other dark, leafy greens for fresh greens. See photo on page 81.

Mango Sauce

This sweet and tangy dish is a good substitute for apple sauce, with a bit more attitude. You can make mango sauce with green or ripe mangoes, but keep in mind that ripe ones are sweeter and easier to peel. Add a bit more sugar if you use green mangoes.

2 mangoes
2 teaspoons lemon juice
½ cup (100 grams) sugar

1. Wash mangoes. Cut a thick slice from each side as close to the seed as possible. Score fruit on each slice with a sharp knife, without cutting through the skin (see photo opposite page). Press inward on skin to turn slice inside out, making scored fruit stand out. Slice fruit from skin. Remove skin from around seed and slice remaining fruit from seed.
2. Cut fruit into small dice. Combine in a medium saucepan with ½ cup (120 milliliters) water, lemon juice, and sugar.
3. Bring mixture to a boil, then simmer slowly over medium-low heat for 30 minutes. Mash occasionally with a spoon or potato masher.
4. Mixture should be thickened and bubbly when you remove from heat. You can finish mashing with a potato masher, or for a smoother texture purée in a food processor or blender.

Yield: 4 servings

Mango sauce

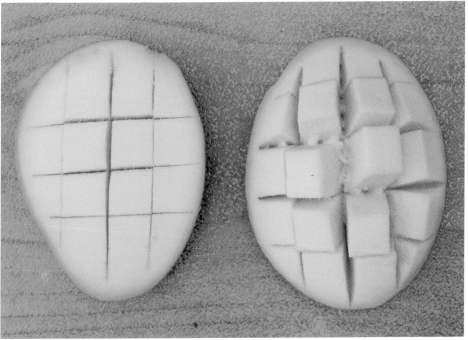

Method for scoring and slicing mango

Liberia and Sierra Leone: Colonizing the Rain Forest

Liberia is one of only two African countries that was never colonized by Europeans (the other country is Ethiopia). In the 1800's the thickly forested Liberian coast was sparsely populated. It was called the Grain Coast because melegueta peppers, also called "grains of paradise," grew there.

The American Colonization Society formed in the early 1800's to resettle freed slaves in Africa, and the Grain Coast was chosen as their destination. The first land was purchased from local Africans for $300 worth of goods. This is the site of Monrovia today. Gradually the settlers acquired more coastal land. In 1847 the various settlements united and took the name Liberia from the latin Liber, meaning *free*.

Sierra Leone means *Lion Mountain*, a name given by the Portuguese in 1462 when they saw the steep mountains rising up from the ocean. In 1833 the British outlawed slavery and began to patrol the seas and capture slave ships. During the American revolution some freed American slaves who were loyalists fled to England. A group of English philanthropists decided to resettle these former slaves along the West African coast, and they chose a trading post at the mouth of the Sierra Leone river. This is the city of Freetown today. When the British began to hold trials for the crews of captured slave ships in Freetown, the population grew. Many of the slaves freed from the captured ships stayed and settled in the area.

Both Liberia and Sierra Leone are heavily forested with monsoon climates. Along the coast the rainfall averages up to 150 inches each year. Five major rivers run through Liberia, making the wet country an ideal place to grow rice, palm and rubber trees.

Bawan damana baturen rani.
Slave during the rains, lord in the dry season.

Starches and Grains

Gari cornmeal fufu

In a typical West African meal a spicy sauce with a sheen of oil is served with a starchy vegetable or grain. This starch has been pounded and cooked until it is thick enough to hold its shape. Bits of it are broken off and dipped in the sauce, and then eaten. The starch makes up the most filling part of the meal, and the sauce is an accent or flavouring. To reflect this style of eating, the serving sizes given here are generous.

This starchy dish may be made from yams, cassava, plantain, green banana, rice or rice flour, beans, millet, sorghum or cornmeal. In southern Nigeria, pounded yams and cassava are used most frequently, and the dish is called *fufu*. Northern Nigerians use grains to make their *tuwo*, which is served the same way. Liberians use rice, easily grown in their wet climate, and also make a mixture called *dumboy* from pounded yams. In Ghana several root vegetables and beans are used to prepare *ampesi*. Ghanians also ferment cornmeal to make *kenkey*, a steamed dumpling with a pungent taste. When the fermented cornmeal is cooked into a thickened paste instead of steaming, it is called *banku*. These foods are always served with a spicy sauce.

Contents

Boiled Rice

Rice is a natural complement for many West African sauces. This recipe is for long-grain white rice. If you prefer to use brown rice or a specialty rice such as Basmati, you will need to adjust your cooking time accordingly.

1½ cups (300 grams) long-grain white rice
3 cups (725 milliliters) water
1 teaspoon salt (optional)

1. Combine rice, water and optional salt in a medium saucepan and bring to a simmer over medium heat.
2. Reduce heat to low, cover and simmer without stirring 12 to 15 minutes.
3. Remove from heat and fluff with a fork. Cover and let sit 5 minutes before serving.

Yield: 4 cups cooked rice

Note: To cook brown rice, increase cooking time to 30 to 40 minutes.

Boiled Plantains

Plantains look like bananas but do not taste like them. They are more like a vegetable than a fruit, and must be cooked before you eat them. Warm plantain slices are often served with a spicy sauce.

4 ripe, unpeeled plantains

1. Scrub plantains thoroughly with soap and water. Rinse. Do not peel plantains.
2. Place plantains in a large pot, cover with water and bring to a boil.
3. Simmer 15 to 20 minutes until plantains are tender enough to be easily pierced with a fork.
4. Remove plantains, and peel them when they are cool enough to handle. This is easily done by cutting through the peel with a sharp knife along the entire length of the plantain, then sliding your fingers under the peel to pull it off.
5. Slice plantains into 1-inch (2½ centimeter) chunks.

Yield: 4 servings

Farina Tuwo

This thick starch has a grainier texture than the glossy potato starch fufu. Tuwo (pronounced too-oh) is often made from sorghum in Northern Nigeria.

2 teaspoons peanut oil
2 cups (400 grams) farina

1. Combine 4 cups (1 liter) water and oil in heavy or non-stick pan, and bring to a boil over medium heat.
2. Pour in farina, stirring constantly. Reduce heat and cook, stirring, about 15 minutes. Mixture will form a soft, stiff dough.
3. Use wet hands to mold fufu into a smooth, rounded shape. Serve with a soup or stew.

Yield: 4 large servings

Boiled plantains

Farina tuwo

Chunky Banana, Plantain and Root Vegetables

In Ghana this dish of many shapes and textures is called ampesi. Use whatever fresh root vegetables are available in your area. Fresh cassava is toxic until it is cooked, so do not nibble ahead of time!

½ pound (250 grams) yam
1 ripe plantain
½ pound (250 grams) cassava (yuca)
1 green (unripe) banana
½ pound (250 grams) sweet or white potato

1. Scrub vegetables with soap and water and rinse. Do not peel vegetables.
2. Place vegetables in a large pot and cover with water. Bring to a boil and simmer over medium heat 15 to 20 minutes, until they are tender enough to be easily pierced with a fork.
3. Remove vegetables from water. Peel them when they are cool enough to handle. The skins should slip off easily. To peel green bananas and plantains cut through the peel lengthwise with a sharp knife.
4. Slice vegetables into 1-inch (2½ centimeter) chunks.

Yield: 4 servings

Gari and Cornmeal Fufu

This fufu has the tangy taste of gari, a flour made from fermented cassava.

1 cup (140 grams) gari
1 cup (150 grams) cornmeal
½ teaspoon salt

1. Mix gari and cornmeal together in a medium sized bowl.
2. Measure 1 cup (240 milliliters) water into a medium sized, heavy or non-stick saucepan. Add the gari mixture and stir into water until smooth.
3. Add 2 cups (475 milliliters) water and the salt and cook over medium heat, stirring with a wooden spoon, 10 minutes. Mixture will gradually thicken. When it is very stiff and forms a thick mass, remove from heat.
4. Use wet hands to mold fufu into a smooth, rounded shape.

Yield: 4 large servings

Note: See photo on page 99.

Yam and Plantain Fufu

Let's face it, there is no quick and easy way to make fufu from fresh yams, but to the fufu connois-seur the effort is well worth it. It helps to have a sizeable mortar and pestle, which is what the African women use to pound their fufu. You can improvise with a sturdy bowl and a large, heavy pounding tool with a flat bottom, such as a spice pestle. This is more than just mashing. You need to really break down the fibers in the yam to allow its sticky, adhesive qualities to shine through. Running the yam through a food mill will also make it smooth. Plantain adds a sweet taste and golden colour to this fufu.

1 pound (500 grams) yam
2 ripe plantains

1. Peel yam and cut into cubes. Place in a medium saucepan, cover with water and bring to a boil. Simmer 15 minutes.
2. While yam is simmering, peel plantain by cutting through the peel lengthwise and running fingers underneath to lift it off. Cut plantain into 1-inch (2½ centimeter) chunks.
3. Add plantain chunks to simmering water. Simmer another 15 minutes until yam and plantain are both very soft.
4. Drain vegetables, and place in large bowl or mortar. Pound until smooth and cohesive with a consistency of firm dough. You can add up to 1 cup (240 milliliters) hot water if necessary. For smoother texture you can pound the vegetables lightly and then grind them through a food mill.
5. Use wet hands to form a smooth, rounded shape on the plate. Serve with a spicy sauce.

Yield: 4 large servings

Mashed Black-eyed Peas with Spices

In Ghana this dish is known as aboboe. It has the smooth texture of mashed potatoes, but with a spicy, nutty taste. You can prepare the black-eyed peas up to two days ahead and refrigerate.

1½ cups (300 grams) dried black-eyed peas, soaked overnight
½ teaspoon ground red pepper
1 teaspoon salt
1 teaspoon sugar
2 tablespoons chopped fresh parsley

1. Remove skins from black-eyed peas. (see Skinning black-eyed peas on page 24)
2. Cover peas with water in a medium saucepan and bring to a boil. Simmer, partially covered, until tender, 30 to 45 minutes.
3. Drain peas. In a food processor or blender, combine peas, red pepper, salt and sugar. Blend until smooth, with a consistency of mashed potatoes. If necessary you can add 2 tablespoons water while blending.
4. Stir in parsley and serve warm, with a spicy sauce.

Yield: 6 servings

Mashed Fried Plantain and Black-eyed Peas

These lively mashed vegetables are called adalu in Ghana. Serve them as you would rice with a spicy sauce, such as Sunday Stew. Be sure to soak your peas overnight and leave about an hour to cook them, unless you are using canned peas. A touch of palm oil gives this dish an exotic flavour.

1 cup (200 grams) dried black-eyed peas, soaked overnight, (or 1 can cooked)
2 ripe plantains (yellow with black spots)
½ teaspoon ground red pepper
1 teaspoon salt
2 tablespoons palm oil (substitute peanut oil if not available)

1. Cover black-eyed peas with water in a medium saucepan and bring to a boil. Simmer about 45 minutes, until very soft. Drain. If you are using canned peas simply drain.
2. Peel plantain by cutting through peel with a sharp knife lengthwise, then sliding fingers under peel to pull it off. Slice in rounds and place in saucepan with enough water to partially cover. Bring to a boil and simmer about 20 minutes, until very soft. Drain.
3. Mash peas and plantains together coarsely in a medium sized bowl. Add red pepper and salt and mix well.
4. Melt oil in medium skillet. Add pea mixture and heat, stirring occasionally, about 10 minutes.

Yield: 4 large servings

Mashed fried plantain and black-eyed peas

Potato starch fufu

Rice balls

Potato Starch Fufu

This recipe is adapted from the "make do fufu" frequently found in older West African cookbooks. Many Africans living in the United States or Europe, unable to get traditional foods, made do with what is available to get as close as possible to those familiar textures and tastes. It is easier these days to find African yams in the northern hemisphere. However, if you can not get them or want an easier recipe, this one will give you the same glossy texture.

¾ cup (20 grams) instant Idaho potato flakes
¾ cup (100 grams) potato starch

1. Measure instant potatoes and starch into bowl and whisk until lumps are gone. Add 4 cups (1 liter) water gradually, stirring until mixture is smooth.
2. Pour mixture into heavy or non-stick pan, and place over low heat. Fill a small bowl with extra water and keep nearby.
3. Cook over low heat, stirring constantly with wooden spoon or flat wooden paddle. Dip spoon in water occasionally to keep mixture from sticking. Add 1 to 2 tablespoons of water if necessary. After about 15 minutes of cooking, fufu will have formed an elastic mass which pulls away from the sides of the pan.
4. Use wet hands to mold fufu into a smooth, rounded shape. Serve with a soup or stew.

Yield: 2 large servings or 4 smaller (to complement rice)

Note: Potato starch is available in many health food or Spanish or African food stores, or by mail order (see Sources). See photo on page 109.

Rice Balls

Pounded rice can be shaped into balls and dipped into a spicy stew. Traditionally this is done with the hands, but you can use silverware if you must. You may also enjoy eating these balls simply with butter, salt and pepper.

1 cup (200 grams) short-grain rice
1 teaspoon salt

1. Combine rice, salt and 3 cups (725 milliliters) water in a heavy or non-stick pan. Bring to a boil, cover and cook over low heat for 15 minutes. Beat occasionally with a wooden spoon – this will release the starch in the rice and make it stickier.
2. Remove from heat and mash rice slightly with a wooden spoon or a potato masher.
3. When rice is cool enough to handle, roll mixture into small balls. Wet hands to prevent rice from sticking.

Yield: 10 rice balls

Note: See photo on page 109.

Rice Tuwo

The Hausa call this tuwo shinkafa. Fine rice flour gives it a smooth consistency without the sticky texture of yams. You can find rice flour at a health food store, or check Sources for mail order companies.

1 teaspoon salt
2 cups (400 grams) rice flour

1. Combine salt and 4 cups (1 liter) water in a heavy or non-stick pan, and bring to a boil.
2. Sprinkle rice flour into water, stirring quickly with a wooden spoon or flat wooden paddle. Reduce heat to low and continue to cook and stir for 10 minutes.
3. Use wet hands to mold tuwo into a smooth, rounded shape. Serve with soup or stew.

Yield: 4 large servings

Imoyo Eba

Imoyo dishes have a Brazilian influence brought over by West African slaves freed from Brazil in the 19th century. Broth, tomato paste and butter make eba one of the tastier versions of the starchy staple dishes common to West Africa. Serve this with chicken imoyo.

2¼ cups (550 milliliters) broth
¼ cup plus 2 tablespoons tomato paste
1½ cups (200 grams) gari or grits
2 tablespoons butter

1. Mix broth and tomato paste in a heavy or non-stick saucepan. Heat until just beginning to boil.
2. Sprinkle gari or grits over broth, stirring vigorously until absorbed. Cook over medium heat for 10 minutes, until stiff. Add an extra ½ cup (125 milliliters) water if you are using grits.
3. Remove from heat. Add butter and mix well. Use wet hands to mold eba into a smooth, rounded shape.

Yield: 4 servings

Kenkey

This sour tasting corn dough needs to ferment for three days. After this it is traditionally wrapped in corn husks and steamed. Serve hot or cold with a spicy sauce. Kenkey goes especially well with fiery pepper sauce.

2½ cups (375 grams) yellow cornmeal
2 cups (475 milliliters) warm water plus 2 cups (475 milliliters) for boiling
1 teaspoon salt
cornhusks for wrapping, soaked in warm water for one hour

1. Pour cornmeal into large bowl, and add the warm water. Mix well to form a soft dough. Leave at room temperature in a covered container for 3 days. Do not stir.
2. Uncover and scrape off any mold which may have formed on top. The mixture will have a very sour smell.
3. Combine salt and 2 cups of water in a medium heavy or non-stick pan, and bring to a boil. Add 2 cups of the cornmeal mixture. Cook, stirring occasionally, 10 minutes. It will become very thick and doughy.
4. Remove dough from heat, and stir or knead in remaining cornmeal mixture. Select six large cornhusks. Tear 12 (½ -inch) lengthwise strips off smaller husks, and tie 2 strips together to make 6 longer strips. You will use these to tie the packets. Place pieces of dough the size of tennis balls (a heaping ½-cup) in the center of each husk. Fold ends over and wrap up tightly into a packet. Tie and seal packets. (See Steaming with cornhusks and banana leaves on page 39)
5. Place a steaming rack in a large pot and fill with water just to the bottom of the rack. Place kenkey bundles on the rack, bring water to a boil and steam, covered, 1 hour.

Yield: 6 servings kenkey

The Dogon of Mali

Two French anthropologists lived with the Dogon people of Mali for a period in the 1950's, and studied their lifestyle and ceremonies. They saw that these people knew an extraordinary amount about the stars and heavens. The Dogon had dances and masks showing the detailed path of Sirius, the Dog-star, and a white dwarf-star in orbit around it. This white dwarf, named Sirius B, could barely be seen through telescopes at the time and was not even photographed until 1970. The Dogon had been tracing its path through masks and ceremonies that dated back hundreds of years.

The Dogon also knew that Jupiter has 4 major moons, and Saturn is surrounded by rings. They knew the earth is round, orbits the sun and rotates on its axis.

How could the Dogon have learned these things without the aid of telescopes and other equipment? They claim to have been taught by extra-terrestrial travelers who visited them on earth thousands of years ago. Some scholars believe they learned through contact with other advanced ancient civilizations. The unanswered questions about this fascinating culture remain.

The Dogon people live in Bandiagara, a 100-mile stretch of sandstone cliffs which runs parallel to the Niger River in eastern Mali, and western Burkina Faso. They build their clay houses right into the cliffs, which have given them some protection from warriors who raided the savannah for centuries. The Dogon farm millet and sorghum on the nearby plains, and store their harvest in granaries which tower above the courtyards of their family compounds.

Kome dadin tuwo ba shi kin mai.

However good the tuwo, it won't refuse fat.

Miya

Sunday Stew

Miya is the Hausa name used in Northern Nigeria for the spicy sauce typically served with a thick, starchy staple. This sauce is often tomato based, with plenty of onions and hot peppers, so that people have been known to exclaim that their mouths are on fire after a taste. It can be made with many combinations of vegetables, chicken, meats, or seafood. You will often find two or three types of meat mingling in one sauce

West Africans use many foods to thicken their sauces. Ground egusi seeds and peanut butter add a rich nutty texture and taste. Agbono, okra and baobab leaves give sauces a slippery consistency which is very popular. Ground or mashed vegetables including tomatoes and onions, pumpkin, eggplant and beans are used often. A purée of tomatoes, onions and peppers is added to sauces so frequently that older West African cookbooks simply refer to the mixture as "the ingredients."

Oil has a special place in the traditional West African diet, and sauces are often covered with its golden luster. Palm oil gives sauces a wonderful red colour and unique taste, and is essential to some of these recipes. Peanut oil is the second most common choice. I've drastically cut the amount of oil in these recipes to reflect our lifestyle and eating habits today. If it still seems like a lot of oil, you can add even less during your cooking.

Contents

Chicken and Meats

Fish and Seafood

Vegetables

The Hausa: The Legend of Bayajida

According to legend, the first seven Hausa city-states were founded by descendants of the son of the King of Baghdad. The King of Baghdad quarreled with his son, Bayajida, and Bayajida set off across the Sahara with an entourage of Arabs, to seek his own fortune. They travelled south through the desert until they reached the kingdom of Bornu, around Lake Chad. Here Bayajida married the King of Bornu's daughter, Magira. The King considered Bayajida a threat to his kingdom and plotted to kill him. Bayajida and Magira discovered the plot and fled into northern Nigeria. Magira was pregnant, and stopped at Biram, where she had a son.

Bayajida went on until he arrived at Daura, and there he stopped and asked an old woman to get him a drink from the well. She replied that the well was guarded by a snake, Sarki, who would only allow them to draw water on Fridays. Bayajida went to the well to draw the water himself. When he lowered the bucket Sarki rose up out of the water, a dreadful serpent with the head of a horse. The man and the serpent struggled and fought. By daybreak, Bayajida killed Sarki and cut off his head.

When the Queen of Daura discovered Bayajida had killed the snake and liberated the town, she offered him anything he desired. He asked for her hand in marriage. They had a son named Bawo, and Bawo's seven sons were the rulers of the first seven Hausa states. These walled cities located throughout Northern Nigeria were named Daura, Biram (founded by Magira's son), Kano, Rano, Gobir, Zaria and Katsina.

Today the ancient well at Daura bears an inscription telling the story of Bayajida. Parts of the old walls and gates of the seven original Hausa cities still stand with the modern cities built up around them. The Hausa people today are farmers, craftsmen and traders living mainly in Nigeria and Niger.

Tuwo na iyali, nama na maigida.
Porridge for the family, meat for the master of the house

Peanut pyramids in Kano, Nigeria. Each pyramid stores 1000 tons of peanuts in bags ready for export

Groundnut chop with toppings

Groundnut Chop

Served over rice, with a selection of fruit and vegetable toppings, this sauce makes a wonderful buffet for a family get-together or casual party. Be sure to use smooth, unsweetened peanut butter.

½ teaspoon salt
½ teaspoon ground ginger
3 pounds (1½ kilograms) chicken pieces, skin removed if desired
2 tomatoes
1 onion
2 fresh hot peppers, chopped and seeded or ½ teaspoon ground red pepper
2 tablespoons peanut oil
1 pound (500 grams) beef, cut in chunks (optional)
1 teaspoon ground crayfish
½ teaspoon salt
½ teaspoon thyme
2 tablespoons tomato paste
½ cup (125 grams) smooth, unsweetened peanut butter
6 hardboiled eggs, peeled

1. Mix salt and ground ginger in a small bowl, and rub thoroughly into chicken pieces on all sides. Cover and leave at room temperature for about 30 minutes.
2. In a food processor or blender grind tomatoes, onion and hot peppers together until smooth. Set aside.
3. Heat oil in a large, heavy or non-stick pan. Add chicken pieces and beef. Brown well on both sides over medium-high heat. Remove and set aside.
4. Add ground vegetables to pan, and simmer for about 15 minutes, uncovered.
5. Add ground red pepper (if using), crayfish, salt, thyme, tomato paste and two cups (475 milliliters) of water. Mix well and bring to a boil.
6. Measure peanut butter into small heat-resistant bowl. Ladle about one cup of broth from the sauce into the bowl, and mix well with peanut butter. Add this paste to the sauce.
7. Return chicken and beef to the pot. Simmer uncovered over medium heat, 30 to 45 minutes, until chicken is fully cooked.
8. Add whole, peeled eggs to sauce during last 10 minutes of cooking. Remove and serve separately with a selection of other toppings. See following page for suggestions.

Yield: 6 servings

Note: See photo on page 119.

Toppings for Groundnut Chop

Any of these toppings will compliment the flavour of groundnut sauce. Choose 2 or 3 toppings for a light meal, or as many as 10 for an elaborate buffet. The cold toppings can be prepared ahead and kept in the refrigerator in small bowls, to be pulled out when dinner is served.

Cold Toppings:

Sliced bananas sprinkled with lemon or orange juice
Chopped tomatoes, or Diced Tomato Salad (recipe page 90)
Chopped green pepper
Sliced cucumber
Fresh coconut, grated (recipe page 62), plain or toasted
Sliced onion sprinkled with vinegar and sugar
Diced pineapple
Chopped, roasted peanuts
Papaya, peeled and cut into cubes, mixed with lemon juice and fresh chili pepper strips
Cool Okra with Spices (recipe page 91)
Avocado, peeled and cut in cubes, mixed with lemon juice, ground ginger and salt to taste
Extra chopped fresh hot peppers for people who like their food fiery
Fresh mango, peeled and cut in chunks
Any type of chutney

Warm Toppings:

Fiery pepper sauce (recipe page 156)
Eggplant, peeled, cubed and fried or boiled
Fried onion rings
Spicy plantain bites (recipe page 27)

Gurbin mai ya fi na ruwa.
A resting place for oil is better than one for water.

Yassa Chicken Breasts with Lemon and Onion

The lemony flavour of this dish is similar to Moroccan cooking, and indeed it is often served in the countries closest to Morocco, such as Senegal and Sierra Leone. The strong flavours of lemon and onion will blend during cooking to make a fragrant and memorable meal. Be sure to leave enough time in your preparation to marinate the chicken for several hours. Serve with check rice.

2 cups (2 large or 4 small) onions, sliced thinly
4 cloves garlic, minced
2 fresh hot peppers, chopped and seeded if desired
½ teaspoon ground ginger
1 teaspoon black pepper
1 tablespoon salt
1 cup (240 milliliters) fresh lemon juice (4 lemons)
1 tablespoon plus another 4 tablespoons peanut oil
2 pounds (2 whole) chicken breasts, split, boned and skinned

1. Combine onions, garlic, hot peppers, ginger, black pepper and salt in a large glass or non-metallic dish.
2. Add lemon juice, 1 cup (240 milliliters) of water, and 1 tablespoon of the oil. Mix well.
3. Add chicken breasts to marinade and arrange so pieces are evenly coated. Marinate 2 hours at room temperature, or longer in the refrigerator.
4. Heat remaining 4 tablespoons of the oil in a heavy pot or skillet. Remove chicken from marinade, reserving marinade. Fry chicken on medium-high heat until well browned on both sides and cooked through, about 30 minutes. Remove from pan and keep covered.
5. Strain marinade through a sieve, reserving both the marinade and the onions.
6. Add the strained onions to skillet and fry over medium heat until golden brown, 10 to 15 minutes. Remove from skillet and keep with chicken.
7. Add ½ cup (120 milliliters) of the strained marinade and ¼ cup (60 milliliters) of water to the skillet. Simmer over medium-high heat for 5 minutes. Spoon sauce over chicken breasts and serve warm.

Yield: 4 servings

Yassa chicken breasts with lemon and onion

Palaver sauce

Chicken Imoyo

Imoyo dishes were introduced to West Africa by freed African slaves returning from Brazil in the 19th century. Some of the new ingredients they brought were olive oil, green peppers and garlic. Imoyo dishes are usually marinated in either vinegar, lemon or lime juice, adding a new dimension to the spicy cooking of the region. You can arrange these chicken pieces and vegetables on a large platter with imoyo eba in the center. The sauce is spicy, citrusy and aromatic. You can substitute lemon juice or vinegar for the lime juice if you prefer.

5 small or 3 large tomatoes
1 roasting chicken, giblets removed
8 ounces (250 grams) okra, fresh or frozen, ends trimmed
5 fresh hot peppers, seeded and cut in strips lengthwise
½ teaspoon ground red pepper
2 cloves garlic, chopped
¼ cup (100 grams) tomato paste
2 tablespoons lime juice
2 tablespoons olive oil
½ teaspoon salt

Serve with imoyo eba-recipe on page 112

1. Cut the tomatoes in quarters and remove seeds with the tip of a sharp knife. Discard seeds.
2. If you want to skin the chicken, it is easiest while it is still whole. Then cut into 8 serving pieces, including 2 breast halves. Discard the backbone and ribs. Remove sharp bones from breast and cut each half into two pieces crosswise.
3. Place chicken in deep pan, add 3 cups (725 milliliters) water and cover. Bring to a boil, then lower heat and simmer 15 minutes, stirring once or twice to make sure the chicken is not sticking to the pan.
4. Add the okra, tomatoes and hot peppers to the pot. Continue to simmer 10 minutes more, until chicken is cooked through but not falling apart.
5. Lift chicken and vegetables out of pot with a slotted spoon and keep warm in a separate pan.
6. Strain 2 cups (475 milliliters) of the broth from pan into a smaller saucepan. Add red pepper, garlic, tomato paste, lime juice, oil and salt. Bring to a boil and simmer 10 minutes, uncovered, over medium heat.
7. Prepare imoyo eba and place in center of a large platter. Arrange chicken pieces and vegetables around eba on platter. Serve sauce in separate bowls for dipping.

Yield: 4 servings

Baked Chicken in Groundnut Sauce

The flavours in this oven-baked dish blend to create a delicious nutty sauce. Use smooth, unsweetened peanut butter.

3 tablespoons peanut oil
3 pounds (1½ kilograms) chicken, cut in pieces, skin removed if desired
1 onion, sliced thinly
4 tomatoes, chopped
1 green bell pepper, seeded and sliced thinly
1 teaspoon thyme
1 bay leaf
1 teaspoon salt
½ teaspoon ground red pepper
1 cup (250 grams) smooth, natural peanut butter
1 cup (240 milliliters) broth
10 ounces (300 grams) whole okra, fresh or frozen

1. Preheat oven to 375°F (190°C).
2. Heat oil in large skillet over medium-high heat and brown chicken pieces on both sides. Arrange chicken in single layer in a large baking dish. Drain extra fat from skillet, leaving about 2 tablespoons.
3. Add onion, tomatoes and green pepper to skillet and simmer 10 minutes over medium heat, until soft. Add thyme, bay leaf, salt and red pepper, mixing well. Arrange vegetables on top of chicken in baking dish.
4. In a small bowl, mix peanut butter and broth until smooth. Pour over chicken and vegetables. Scatter okra over chicken.
5. Cover chicken and bake 45 minutes. Uncover and bake another 15 minutes. Add more stock or water during baking for extra sauce. Serve with rice.

Yield: 4 generous servings

The Fulani

These nomadic herdsmen are a mysterious people. They look different from other West Africans; they are tall and slim with sharp features, aquiline noses, straight or wavy hair and sometimes even blue eyes. Records show the Fulani people lived in the Senegal River Valley around the 10th century, and moved west until they reached northern Nigeria and Hausaland about 500 years later. They may have migrated to Senegal from Morocco or Arabia, or they could even be descendants of the Asiatic people of East Africa.

The Fulani, also called Fulbe or Peul, gradually spread over most of the West African savannah, trading milk, meat and hides for grains, vegetables and household wares. In the early 19th century Usman dan Fodio, a Muslim Fulani chief, led a holy war against the Hausa cities. He replaced the Hausa rulers with Fulani emirs, and set up his center of rule in Sokoto, a city now in present day Nigeria. Trade began to thrive under the security the Fulani government offered. Kano in particular grew as camel caravans passed through daily on their way to and from the desert.

Fulani seem to have natural leadership and organizational skills. The shepherds have the remarkable ability to recognize each animal in a herd of hundreds of cattle. Many Fulani who break from their traditional way of life and settle in towns quickly occupy important positions in their societies.

Tuwan girma miya tasa da nama a kye yi.

The important person's tuwo, its gravy is made with meat.

photo by Thadd Jackson

Fulani boys on a hillside at Miango, Nigeria

Red palm oil

Egusi

Palaver Sauce

Palaver comes from the Portuguese word "palavra" which means a word, or speech. During colonial times a negotiation between Africans and Europeans was called a palaver. Today this word can mean any type of lengthy discussion. Some countries such as Mali even have a palaver tree, a shady spot designated for gathering and hashing out the affairs of the community. The palaver sauce recipe always has many different meats and vegetables, as if a whole town got together and threw all their leftovers into the pot. Perhaps this sultry, spicy mixture simmered during a long village palaver, to be enjoyed by the whole community when the discussions were over. Many hungry people might gather around the pot as it cooked, adding their own advice and ingredients,and starting a palaver of their own. Use palm oil for this sauce if available – it adds a lovely red colour. Serve with fufu or rice balls.

½ cup (120 milliliters) peanut or palm oil
½ pound (250 grams) beef, cut in chunks
3 pounds (1½ kilograms) chicken, cut in pieces, skin removed if desired
1 onion, thinly sliced
2 tomatoes, chopped
1 teaspoon curry powder
½ teaspoon ground red pepper, or to taste
½ teaspoon salt
1 tablespoon ground crayfish
5 ounces (150 grams) okra, stemmed and sliced crosswise
½ pound (250 grams) mixed greens such as kale or spinach, stemmed and chopped (4 to 5 cups)
¼ pound (125 grams) fresh mushrooms, sliced
½ pound (250 grams) lean or fat fish fillets, raw or previously steamed or baked

1. Heat oil in large, heavy or non-stick pot and cook beef and chicken over medium-high heat until brown on both sides. Remove from pot and set aside.
2. Add onion, tomatoes, curry powder, red pepper, salt and dried crayfish to pot. Simmer 20 minutes on medium to low heat.
3. Add 3 cups (725 milliliters) water to pot and bring to a boil. Add okra, greens, and mushrooms. Simmer, uncovered, on medium-high heat for 10 minutes.
4. Return meat and chicken to pot, lower heat to medium and simmer, uncovered, 15 minutes.
5. Cut fish into about 8 large chunks, and add to pot. Simmer another 15 minutes, uncovered, until chicken and fish are both cooked through.

Yield: 6 large servings

Note: You can substitute 5 ounces (150 grams) frozen or 2 cups cooked greens for fresh greens. See photo on page 123.

Egusi with Beef

Egusi is a ground melon seed which adds a nut-like texture and flavour to this sauce. Serve with yams or boiled rice.

½ cup (120 milliliters) palm oil, or peanut oil
2 onions, sliced
2 pounds (1 kilogram) beef, cut in chunks
½ cup (200 grams) tomato paste
1 cup (140 grams) egusi seed, ground
½ pound (250 grams) fresh spinach or kale, stemmed and chopped (4 cups)
2–3 fresh hot peppers, seeded and chopped
½ teaspoon ground red pepper
2 cups (300 grams) fresh or frozen okra (10 ounce package frozen)
2 teaspoons ground crayfish
1 teaspoon salt

1. Melt oil over medium-high heat in a large, heavy or non-stick pan. Add onions and beef, and simmer 10 minutes, until beef is browned.
2. Add tomato paste, egusi, and 3 cups (725 milliliters) water.
3. Add spinach or kale, fresh hot peppers, ground red pepper, okra, ground crayfish and salt. Bring to a slow boil, reduce heat and simmer 30 to 45 minutes covered. Stir occasionally, adding a small amount of water if it becomes too thick.

Yield: 6 servings

Variation: **Egusi with Fish** – Follow recipe above, but omit beef. Add 1 pound fresh fish fillets during final 10 minutes of cooking. Cover and simmer 10 minutes, or until fish begins to flake.

Note: You can use 5 ounces (150 grams) frozen or 3 cups fresh spinach or kale for fresh greens. You can purchase egusi in most African food stores.

Red Palm Oil Sauce with Chicken, Beef and Pork

You must use palm oil to get the rich, deep taste and colour of this sauce. However, you can substitute many different kinds of meats or vegetables. The version below comes from Sierra Leone.

1 cup (240 milliliters) red palm oil (do not substitute other oils)
1 whole chicken, skin removed if desired, and cut in pieces
½ pound (250 grams) beef, cut in chunks
½ pound (250 grams) pork, cut in chunks, or 1 pigs foot, soaked and chopped
2 onions, coarsely chopped
3 fresh hot peppers, coarsely chopped
½ teaspoon ground red pepper
1 teaspoon salt
½ teaspoon thyme
6 tablespoons (150 grams) tomato paste

1. Heat oil in large, heavy or non-stick pan and cook chicken pieces over medium-high heat until brown on both sides, about 15 minutes. Remove and set aside.
2. Add beef and pork chunks to the pot and cook on same heat until brown, about 10 minutes.
3. Grind onions and fresh hot peppers in a blender or food processor until smooth. Add to meat and simmer 5 minutes, until heated through.
4. Add red pepper, salt, thyme, tomato paste, and 1 cup (240 milliliters) water. Stir until smooth.
5. Return chicken to pot. Simmer about 30 minutes on medium heat, uncovered, until chicken is cooked through. Serve with rice or fufu.

Yield: 6 servings

Beef with Hot Pepper and Mushrooms

Mushrooms give an earthy flavour to this savory sauce. Because it is thickened with flour it does not require as much simmering as some of the other recipes. It is delicious served over rice.

½ cup (75 grams) white flour
1 teaspoon salt
½ teaspoon ground red pepper, or to taste
1 pound (500 grams) beef, cut in chunks
1 pound (500 grams) fresh white mushrooms, large ones sliced, and small ones left whole
¼ cup (60 milliliters) peanut oil
1 tomato, chopped
1 onion, chopped

1. Mix flour, salt, and red pepper in a medium bowl or a zip-lock bag. Add beef chunks to flour mixture and stir or shake to cover. Remove beef and repeat process with mushrooms. Remove mushrooms and save leftover flour.
2. Heat oil in large, heavy or non-stick pan. Add beef and cook over medium-high heat until browned, about 10 minutes.
3. Add tomato and onion. Continue to simmer over medium heat for 10 minutes.
4. Add leftover flour mixture and cook 5 minutes, stirring.
5. Add 1½ cups (360 milliliters) water and stir until smooth. Simmer on low heat, covered, 15 to 20 minutes.
6. Add mushrooms. Simmer 15 minutes more.

Yield: 4 servings

Beef with Agbono, Tomato and Greens

Agbono seeds, also called apon, are used to thicken West African sauces and get that slippery texture which is so popular in this cuisine. If you are using a very salty type of fish such as smoked herring, soak in cold water for several hours, rinse and drain before using.

½ cup (120 milliliters) palm oil
½ pound (250 grams) beef, pork or other red meat, cut in chunks
1 onion, thinly sliced
1 tablespoon tomato paste
½ teaspoon ground red pepper
½ teaspoon salt
2 ounces (60 grams) kale or other greens, stemmed and chopped (1 cup)
¼ cup (50 grams) fresh or frozen okra, stemmed and sliced crosswise in thin slices
½ pound (250 grams) dry smoked fish
2 ounces (60 grams) ground agbono seeds
1 tablespoon ground crayfish

1. Heat palm oil in a large, heavy or non-stick pan until melted. Add beef or other meat and simmer in oil over medium-high heat until cooked through.
2. Add sliced onion, tomato paste, red pepper and salt. Continue to simmer 10 minutes over medium heat.
3. Add kale, okra, smoked fish, agbono seeds and crayfish. Simmer mixture for another 5 minutes, until heated through.
4. Add 2 cups (475 milliliters) of water. Bring to a boil and cook over medium heat for another 20 minutes, uncovered, adding more water if necessary. Serve with fufu.

Yield: 4 large servings

Note: You can substitute ½ cup cooked or frozen kale for fresh kale. You can purchase ground agbono at most stores which sell Nigerian foods. If it is not available, you can increase the amount of okra to 1 cup (160 grams).

Liver in Mild Tomato Sauce

West Africans are very efficient cooks, meat is not plentiful, and no part of the animal goes to waste. Organ meats, also known as variety meats or offal, are often on the menu. This delicious recipe is milder than most, and if you want more spice you can add some ground red pepper. Try it with chicken livers too, or substitute your favorite variety meat.

1 pound (500 grams) liver, fresh or frozen
¼ cup (60 milliliters) peanut oil
2 onions, sliced
2 tomatoes, sliced
½ teaspoon thyme
½ cup (200 grams) tomato paste
1 teaspoon salt
½ teaspoon black pepper

1. Slice liver thinly, and then cut lengthwise into stripes about ¼ inch (½ centimeter) wide. Season with salt and pepper.
2. Heat oil in a large skillet. Add liver strips and fry over medium-high heat until browned, turning gently. Remove from pan and keep warm.
3. Add onions and tomatoes to skillet and simmer over medium heat 10 minutes.
4. Stir thyme, tomato paste, salt and pepper into skillet. Continue to cook 5 minutes more, until heated through.
5. Return liver to skillet, and simmer over low-medium heat 15 minutes more. Mixture will be thick. Serve with rice.

Yield: 4 servings

Liver with Tomato and Red Pepper

Organ meats, also called variety meats or offal, are served often in West Africa. This is a spicier way to prepare liver, and you can substitute kidneys, tongue, tripe or any other variety meat that you like.

1 onion, half thinly sliced and half coarsely chopped
3 tomatoes, coarsely chopped
⅓ cup (75 milliliters) peanut oil
1 pound (500 grams) fresh or frozen liver, thinly sliced
½ teaspoon ground red pepper
¼ teaspoon thyme
¼ teaspoon coriander
½ teaspoon salt

1. Grind the coarsely chopped onion with the tomatoes in a blender or food processor until smooth.
2. Heat oil in a large, heavy skillet and fry liver over medium-high heat until well-browned. Remove from skillet and set aside.
3. Add the sliced onion to the same skillet and fry until it is soft, about 5 minutes.
4. Add ground vegetables, red pepper, thyme, coriander and salt to onion in skillet. Bring to a boil and simmer 20 minutes over low-medium heat, covered, stirring occasionally. Add a small amount of water if necessary to prevent sticking.
5. Return liver to skillet and heat through. Serve hot with rice or baked potato.

Yield: 4 servings

Okra with Chicken and Beef

Okra gives this sauce a slippery consistency which is very desirable in West African cuisine. The smaller you chop the okra, the more slippery your sauce will be. Sometimes ground okra can be found in stores or catalogs – this has a very strong taste and produces a sauce which is almost like a gel, so use it sparingly! If you leave the okra whole or simply remove the stems, your sauce will not be as slippery. Slicing the okra in ½-inch (1½ centimeter) rounds makes a nice sauce. If you are using a salty smoked fish such as herring, soak in cold water for several hours, then rinse and drain before beginning recipe.

¼ cup (60 milliliters) peanut or palm oil
6 to 8 chicken pieces
½ pound (250 grams) beef, cut in chunks
1 onion, sliced
½ teaspoon salt
2 tomatoes, sliced
1 tablespoon ground crayfish
1 teaspoon Maggi Sauce or daddawa
2 tablespoons tomato paste
½ teaspoon ground red pepper
10 ounces (300 grams) okra, stemmed and sliced in ½-inch rounds
½ pound (250 grams) dried smoked fish (optional), soaked several hours and drained

1. Heat oil in large, heavy pan. Add chicken and beef and fry over medium-high heat until brown on all sides, about 15 minutes. Remove from pan and set aside.
2. If a lot of fat has accumulated in the pan, you can discard some of it. Add onion, salt and tomatoes. Continue to simmer for 10 minutes.
3. Add ground crayfish, Maggi sauce, tomato paste, red pepper and 3 cups (725 milliliters) water. Bring to a boil. Return chicken and beef to pan.
4. Add okra and optional smoked fish. Simmer 30 minutes, uncovered, until chicken is cooked through. Serve with rice, fufu, or boiled plantains.

Yield: 4 large servings

Note: Maggi Sauce can be purchased in the soup section of most stores, or by mail order (see Sources). You can substitute a liquid bouillon if Maggi Sauce is not available.

Sunday Stew

Sunday is often a day when people relax and gather over a special meal, such as this rich, red sauce served with rice, fufu or mashed beans and plantains. The ground vegetables give it a smooth, silky texture. It is usually served fiery hot, but you can adjust the spices to your taste.

½ cup (125 milliliters) peanut or palm oil
2 pounds (1 kilogram) beef, cut in chunks
2 onions, 1 sliced and 1 coarsely chopped
½ teaspoon thyme
½ teaspoon salt
½ teaspoon ground red pepper
3 large tomatoes, coarsely chopped
¼ cup (100 grams) tomato paste
1 teaspoon Maggi Sauce or daddawa

1. Heat oil in a large, heavy pot. Add beef, sliced onion, thyme, salt and red pepper. Simmer over medium-high heat until meat is browned, about 10 minutes.
2. Grind the coarsely chopped onion and tomatoes in a blender or food processor until smooth.
3. Add ground vegetables, tomato paste and Maggi Sauce to meat. Cook for another 45 minutes, over low to medium heat, uncovered.

Yield: 4 servings

Variation: **Sunday Stew with Fish –** You can substitute 1 pound (500 grams) fresh fish, filleted, for the meat. Cut the fillets in 3 or 4 pieces. Add during the final 10 minutes of cooking, then cover and cook until fish is opaque and beginning to flake.

Note: Maggi Sauce can be purchased in the soup section of most grocery stores, or by mail order (see Sources). You can substitute a liquid bouillon if Maggi Sauce is not available. See photo on page 115.

The Ashanti: Kingdom of Gold

In the 18th century a golden stool is said to have fallen from heaven into the lap of Ashanti King Osei Tutu. The stool became a symbol of power and divine rule for the people of this rare empire of the rain forest. Neither the king nor the stool was allowed to touch the ground; during ceremonies the stool was placed upon another stool. It was not used as a chair, but as an altar. The stool, with its unique bow-shaped seat, is still an important craft and status symbol in Ghana today.

King Osei Tutu's priest was named Ofkomfo Anokye. He planted two trees in the forest, and predicted that one would live and become the capital of Ashantiland, and the other would die. The tree that lived is the site of Kumasi, the Ashanti capital today, which means *the tree lived*. The site of the other tree is Kumawu, which means *the tree died*.

Kente cloth is a beautiful Ashanti creation, traditionally woven from silk by the men. The intricate and colourful patterns symbolize virtues such as courage, creativity, democracy, family unity, mutual sharing, military prowess and divine beauty. This costly cloth was once worn only by royalty.

The glittering wealth of this gold mining region was often displayed in royal ceremonies. Crowns, scepters, breastplates, jewelry and even hats and sandals were covered with gold. The British captured Ashantiland in 1873, and during the struggle that followed many of the magnificent gold artifacts, including the golden stool, were taken. You can see lots of Ashanti gold in the British Museum in London. The Ashanti were defeated and became part of the British Gold Coast Colony in 1901.

Today the Ashanti are part of Ghana, the first African country to gain its independence from Britain in 1957. The name of Ghana was taken after the ancient empire of the same name.

Karyar kada ta ruwa che in ya fito tudu ya zama nama.

The boasting of the crocodile belongs in the water, if it comes on dry ground it becomes meat.

Eggplant Sauce with Fish

Ntorewafroe, as this dish is known in Ghana, has many variations, but always uses eggplant. Serve with rice or mashed black-eyed peas.

> **2 tablespoons peanut oil**
> **2 tablespoons palm oil (or increase peanut oil to 4 tablespoons)**
> **1 onion, chopped**
> **1 green pepper, chopped**
> **1 medium eggplant, about 1½ pounds (750 grams), peeled and cubed**
> **2 large tomatoes, chopped**
> **1 cup (250 milliliters) broth**
> **½ teaspoon salt**
> **½ teaspoon ground red pepper**
> **1 pound (500 grams) fresh fish, filleted and cut in 4 pieces**

1. Heat oils in large, heavy or non-stick pan until palm oil is melted. Add onion and green peppers, and cook over medium heat 5 minutes.
2. Add eggplant and continue to cook 15 minutes, stirring occasionally.
3. Add tomatoes, broth, salt and red pepper. Simmer 15 minutes more, uncovered, over medium heat.
4. Add fish, cover and simmer 10 minutes or until fish is opaque and begins to flake.

Yield: 4 servings

Eggplant Sauce with Shrimp

This spicy version of the popular eggplant sauce is called sesew-froe in Ghana. It uses shrimp instead of fish.

　　1 medium eggplant, about 1½ pounds (750 grams) peeled and cubed
　　1 teaspoon salt
　　2 tomatoes, coarsely chopped
　　1 bunch scallions, coarsely chopped
　　2 fresh hot peppers, seeded and coarsely chopped
　　2 tablespoons peanut oil
　　1 pound (500 grams) shrimp, uncooked, peeled
　　1 cup (250 milliliters) fish stock (broth) or clam juice
　　½ teaspoon salt
　　½ teaspoon ground ginger
　　2 tablespoons tomato paste
　　4 tablespoons chopped fresh parsley

1. Cover eggplant with water in a medium saucepan. Add 1 teaspoon salt, bring to a boil, and cook until eggplant is tender, about 10 minutes. Drain and set aside.
2. In a blender or food processor, grind tomatoes, scallions and hot peppers together.
3. Heat oil in a large, heavy or non-stick pan, add ground vegetables and cook over medium heat 10 minutes.
4. Add shrimp and fish stock to ground vegetables. Bring to a boil, then lower heat and simmer, covered, 10 minutes.
5. Add ½ tsp salt, ginger, tomato paste, parsley and eggplant. Simmer 10 minutes more.

Yield: 4 servings

Shrimp and Okra with Plantains

This dish probably originated in the coastal rainforest where seafood and okra are plentiful. Plantains add texture to this light sauce with a hint of lime flavouring. Use a ripe plantain – it should be completely yellow with black spots.

1 ripe plantain
½ cup (120 milliliters) peanut oil
1 onion, chopped
2 tomatoes, chopped
1 pound (500 grams) okra, fresh or frozen, stemmed and sliced crosswise
1 pound (500 grams) raw shrimp, peeled
½ teaspoon salt
½ teaspoon ground red pepper
¼ teaspoon black pepper
2 tablespoons lime juice (1 lime)
1 cup (125 milliliters) fish stock (broth) or clam juice

1. Peel plantain by making several slits through the skin with a sharp knife, the entire length of the plantain, then pulling skin off with fingers. Slice into ½-inch (1½ centimeter) rounds.
2. Heat oil in a large, heavy pan, add onion and cook over medium heat 10 minutes.
3. Add tomatoes, okra and plantain slices. Continue to cook another 10 minutes.
4. Add shrimp, salt, red and black pepper, lime juice, and the fish stock. Simmer 30 minutes, uncovered, adding more water or stock if necessary. Serve with rice, or kenkey.

Yield: 4 servings

Fish with Coconut Milk

This dish is so easy to prepare, yet elegant enough to be served to guests. Red pepper and kale add colour and spice to the creamy coconut milk sauce. Be sure to use pure, unsweetened coconut milk. Check rice is a colourful complement for the fish.

1½ cup (360 milliliters) canned coconut milk, shaken well to distribute cream
½ teaspoon ground red pepper
1 tablespoon butter
1½ pounds (750 grams) lean, white fish such as haddock, filleted
2 ounces (60 grams) leafy greens such as kale, stemmed and chopped (1 cup)

1. In a large skillet, combine coconut milk, red pepper and butter. Bring to a boil, lower heat and simmer, covered, about 30 minutes. Stir occasionally.
2. Cut fish fillets into 3 or 4 large pieces and add to skillet. Add kale. Simmer on medium heat, covered, until fish is opaque and begins to flake, about 10 minutes.
3. Serve fish and sauce immediately.

Yield: 4 servings

Note: You can substitute ½ cup cooked or frozen leafy greens for fresh greens.

Fish with Ginger

This fried fish sizzles with spices. Serve it with check rice or plain, boiled rice.

¼ teaspoon salt
½ teaspoon ground red pepper
2 teaspoons ground ginger
1 small onion, finely minced
1½ pounds (750 grams) fresh fish, a lean variety such as haddock, filleted
¼ cup (60 milliliters) peanut oil

1. Mix salt, red pepper, ginger and minced onion in a large, flat dish such as a pie plate. Cut fish fillets into 3 or 4 pieces. Coat fish with spice mixture and leave for 30 minutes at room temperature, or longer in the refrigerator. You can also combine spices in a zip-lock bag, add fish, shake to coat and leave in bag to marinate.
2. Heat oil in a large skillet for several minutes, until very hot but not smoking. Add fish and onion mixture and fry on medium-high heat until cooked through, about 5 minutes per side.

Yield: 4 servings

Fish with ginger served with check rice

Seafood salad imoyo served with boiled yams

Smoked herring with tomato and greens, served with boiled plantains

Smoked Herring with Tomato and Greens

This smoky, spicy sauce, called kentumere in Ghana, can be served with rice or boiled plantain.

1 large tomato, coarsely chopped
½ cup (120 milliliters) palm oil or peanut oil, or a mixture of the two
1 large onion, chopped
½ teaspoon ground red pepper
1 cup (100 grams) or 2 tins (3.25 ounces each) kippered herring
½ pound (250 grams) fresh greens such as kale or spinach, stemmed and chopped (4 to 5 cups)

1. Grind tomato in food processor or blender until smooth.
2. Heat oil in a large skillet. Add onion and red pepper and cook over medium heat until onion is soft, about 10 minutes.
3. Add ground tomato and herring and continue to cook for 10 minutes.
4. Add greens and simmer over medium-low heat 15 minutes more, covered.

Yield: 4 servings

Note: You can substitute 6 ounces (175 grams) frozen or 2 cups cooked greens for fresh greens. See photo on page 143.

Seafood Salad Imoyo

This light blend of seafood and spices, served at room temperature, is perfect for a summer lunch. You can substitute different types of seafood such as lobster or scallops for the fish and shrimp. Serve with fried yam chips, boiled yams or boiled plantains.

¾ pound (375 grams) lean, white fish such as haddock, filleted
½ pound (250 grams) uncooked medium shrimp, shelled and deveined
1 tomato
1 green or red bell pepper, seeded and sliced into very thin strips
1 tablespoon chopped fresh parsley
2 fresh hot peppers, chopped
2 cloves garlic, chopped
¼ cup (60 milliliters) lemon or lime juice
2 tablespoons olive oil
1 tablespoon tomato paste
½ teaspoon salt

1. Fill a large skillet with water to about 1 inch (2½ centimeters) deep. Cover and bring to a simmer over medium heat. Add fish fillets and simmer 5 minutes, or until they are opaque and just beginning to flake. Remove fish gently with a slotted spatula, letting water drain, and place fish in a large bowl. Add shrimp to water in skillet and simmer about 5 minutes until cooked through. Remove shrimp with slotted spoon, letting water drain, and add to fish in the bowl.
2. Strain stock from skillet, and reserve ⅔ cup (160 milliliters). You can discard the rest or save for another use.
3. Peel tomato by dropping in boiling water for 1 minute, then running under cold water. The skins should slip off easily. Cut in quarters and scoop out seeds with the tip of a sharp knife. Discard seeds.
4. Chop tomato and mix with green or red pepper, parsley, hot peppers and garlic. Add these vegetables to the fish and shrimp, and mix gently.
5. In a small saucepan, whisk lemon juice, olive oil, tomato paste and salt together. Add the reserved fish stock. Bring to a boil and simmer 5 minutes, uncovered.
6. Pour sauce over fish and vegetable mixture and stir gently. Let stand at room temperature 30 minutes before serving.

Yield: 4 servings

Note: See photo on page 143.

Fish with Hot Peppers

This satisfying dish is very easy to prepare. If you like it really hot, leave the seeds in the peppers when you chop them.

3 tablespoons peanut or palm oil
3 or 4 fresh hot peppers, seeded and minced
2 tablespoons tomato paste
1 small onion, chopped
½ teaspoon salt
1½ pounds (750 grams) lean, white fish such as haddock, filleted

1. Heat oil in large skillet. Add hot peppers, tomato paste, onion and salt and simmer over medium heat 10 minutes.
2. Add fish to skillet, cover and cook over low heat 5 to 10 minutes, until fish is opaque and begins to flake. Serve immediately with rice or fufu.

Yield: 4 servings

Fish with Lime and Tomato

Stronger tasting, fat types of fish, such as bluefish, butterfish or salmon, work well in this aggressive sauce. You can also use a lean fish like haddock. Serve with rice or chunky root vegetables.

1½ pounds (750 grams) fresh lean or fat fish, filleted
½ teaspoon salt
1 tablespoon lime juice
1 tomato, coarsely chopped
1 small onion, coarsely chopped
2 tablespoons peanut oil
1 tablespoon tomato paste
½ teaspoon ground red pepper
⅛ teaspoon cloves

1. Place fish fillets in flat pan in a single layer. Sprinkle with salt and lime juice. Let them stand while you prepare the other ingredients.
2. Grind tomato and onion together in blender or food processor until smooth.
3. Heat oil in large skillet. Sauté onion and tomato mixture over medium heat 5 minutes.
4. Add tomato paste, red pepper, cloves and 1 cup (240 milliliters) water. Simmer, uncovered, 20 minutes.
5. Add fish fillets, and continue to cook, uncovered, about 10 minutes, or until fish is opaque and beginning to flake.

Yield: 4 servings

Fish with Pepper and Yam

This rich red broth abundant with yams and fish is known as pepper soup throughout West Africa. Like chicken soup, it is good for what ails you, and it is often served to pregnant women, or a person with no appetite.

> **1 pound (500 grams) fresh lean or fat fish, filleted**
> **1 tablespoon lime juice**
> **½ teaspoon salt**
> **3 fresh hot peppers, seeded and minced or ground**
> **1 tablespoon tomato paste**
> **1 onion, coarsely chopped**
> **1 tablespoon palm oil or peanut oil**
> **1 pound (500 grams) yams, peeled and cut in cubes.**

1. Place fish in a glass or other non-metallic dish in a single layer, sprinkle with lime juice and salt and marinate 30 minutes at room temperature, or longer if refrigerated.
2. Combine peppers, tomato paste, onion and palm oil with 2 cups (475 milliliters) water in a medium saucepan. Bring to a boil, lower heat and simmer for 30 minutes, covered.
3. Strain mixture into a large skillet, pressing down on vegetables with the back of a spoon to extract liquid. Discard chopped vegetables. Add yams to skillet. Cover and simmer over low-medium heat until yams are soft, about 10 minutes.
4. Add fish to skillet, along with any liquid that has accumulated in dish while marinating. Simmer over low-medium heat, covered, about 10 minutes, or until fish is opaque and begins to flake.
5. Place yams and fish in a serving bowl and spoon sauce over.

Yield: 4 servings

Variation: **Smoked Fish with Pepper and Yam** – Use smoked fish in place of fresh fish. Do not use the lime juice or salt, and omit step 1 (marinating the fish). If you are using smoked herring, soak it in water at least one hour before preparing recipe, drain and rinse, to remove excess salt. Add smoked fish to sauce along with the yams, in step 3. Simmer 20 minutes. Omit step 4.

Smoked Fish with Black-eyed Peas

Be sure to start this recipe early enough, to give yourself time to soak and cook the black-eyed peas and the fish. Serve this strong, spicy sauce with rice, fufu or kenkey.

½ cup (100 grams) dried black-eyed peas, soaked overnight, or 1 can black-eyed peas
½ pound (250 grams) dried smoked fish, bones removed
¼ cup (60 milliliters) palm oil or peanut oil
1 onion, chopped
½ teaspoon ground red pepper
1 tablespoon tomato paste
1 teaspoon Maggi sauce or daddawa

1. If you are using dried peas, cover with water in a medium saucepan and bring to a boil. Simmer until tender, about 1 hour. Set aside. If using canned peas, simply drain and set aside.
2. Cover dried fish with water and simmer 45 minutes, until soft. If you are using a salty smoked fish such as smoked herring, you may not need to soften it, but soak for at least 2 hours and then drain to remove excess salt.
3. Heat oil in large skillet. Add onions, ground pepper, tomato paste and Maggi sauce. Simmer 30 minutes on low heat, uncovered, stirring occasionally.
4. Add smoked fish and black-eyed peas. Simmer another 15 minutes.

Yield: 4 servings

Note: Maggi Sauce can be purchased in the soup section of most stores, or by mail order (see Sources). You can substitute liquid bouillon if Maggi Sauce is not available.

Smoked Fish with Tomato and Yam

The distinctive tastes of palm oil, ground crayfish and smoked fish make this a very exotic and spicy dish. It is guaranteed to wake up your tastebuds, and will appeal more to adventurous eaters or those who are already familiar with African flavours. If you are using a salty fish such as smoked herring, soak it for several hours to remove excess salt. Rinse and drain.

2 onions
2 pounds (1 kilogram) yams, peeled and cubed
½ teaspoon salt
2 tomatoes, coarsely chopped
5 tablespoons tomato paste
½ teaspoon ground red pepper
3 tablespoons palm oil
2 teaspoons ground crayfish or 2 whole dried shrimps
1 teaspoon maggi sauce or daddawa
¼ pound (125 grams) dried smoked fish, soaked

1. Thinly slice one onion, and coarsely chop the other.
2. Heat 1½ cups (360 milliliters) of water in a large, heavy or non-stick pan and add yams, sliced onion, and salt. Bring to a boil.
3. Combine coarsely chopped onion and tomato in a blender or food processor and blend until smooth.
4. To boiling yams add tomato and onion purée, tomato paste, red pepper, palm oil, ground crayfish and maggi sauce. Bring to a boil and simmer, uncovered, over low-medium heat until yam is soft, about 15 minutes.
5. Remove 2 large spoonfuls of the yam with a slotted spoon, draining off the liquid, and mash on a plate. Return mashed yam to the sauce.
6. Stir in smoked fish and simmer 20 minutes more, until sauce is very thick.

Yield: 4 servings

Note: Maggi Sauce can be purchased in the soup section of most stores, or by mail order (see Sources). You can substitute liquid bouillon if Maggi Sauce is not available.

Red Palm Oil Sauce with Fish and Vegetables

You must use red palm oil to get the unique colour and flavour of this sauce. This recipe would traditionally use about 2 cups (475 milliliters) of palm oil. Since this seems like an alarming amount of oil in today's society which strives to be low fat, I suggest a much smaller amount. For a really decadent dish, use the full amount of palm oil. This sauce is delicious with fufu, boiled yams, or rice.

½ cup (120 milliliters) palm oil (do not substitute any other oil)
2 onions, chopped
½ teaspoon ground red pepper
3 tomatoes, chopped
4 ounces (125 grams) okra, fresh or frozen, stemmed and sliced crosswise
1 small eggplant, about 1 pound (500 grams), peeled and cubed
½ teaspoon salt
1 pound (500 grams) lean fish fillets or cooked crab meat

1. Heat palm oil in heavy pan until melted and just beginning to boil. Add onions and red pepper and cook over medium heat, stirring, 10 minutes.
2. Add tomatoes, okra, eggplant, and salt. Simmer 45 minutes, covered, until vegetables are soft and sauce is thickened. Mash vegetables occasionally with spoon during cooking. Add ½ to 1 cup water.
3. Add fish fillets or crab meat, cover, and cook until fish is opaque and begins to flake, 5 to 10 minutes. Crab meat should just be cooked until heated through.

Yield: 4 servings

Variation: **Red Palm Oil Sauce with Beef or Chicken –** Instead of fish, use 1 pound (500 grams) beef, cut in chunks, or 1 chicken cut in pieces. In step 1, brown beef or chicken in oil and remove. Add onions and peppers to oil and continue with recipe. Return meats to the pan after adding the ingredients in step 2, then be sure to simmer until chicken is cooked through. Omit step 3. You can also use a combination of beef and chicken.

The Ibo, the Yoruba and Benin City

The dense rainforests covering most of the West African coast provided a shelter from warriors who raided the desert and savannah. Along with this security came isolation. Many rainforest kingdoms were loose family groups living under separate leaders. Most did not unite to form the powerful empires of the north. Yams and palm oil were the staples here, and clearing the forests for farming was an immense task. Cocoyams, greens, seeds, hot peppers, bananas and wild game supplemented the diet.

In Southwestern Nigeria, the Yoruba city of Ife dates back over 800 years. According to myth this is where Oduduwa, their founding father, created the Yoruba race. Ife has always been a spiritual center for the Yoruba. The city of Oyo began to develop in the 14th century and became the center of military power. All the independent Yoruba kingdoms gave allegiance to the alafin, or king of Oyo. The people of Oyo had a great advantage over their forest neighbors – they were the only people in the area to use horses, which they bought for a steep price from Saharan traders. Like other coastal people, the Yoruba grew prosperous from the Atlantic trade after Europeans discovered the West African coast. Today the Yoruba nation in Nigeria numbers over 25 million. Yoruba are famous for their intricate crafts, including woodcarving and beadwork. Traditionally, all beadwork was created for the king, as with the kente cloth of the Ashanti people. Only the Oba, a direct descendant of Oduduwa, was permitted to wear a sacred beaded crown and slippers.

To the east of Yorubaland, the Edo people built Benin City, one of the largest kingdoms of the forest belt. According to legend the Edo asked Oduduwa, the Yoruba king of Ife, to send them a leader. Oduduwa sent his son Oranmiyan to Benin. Oranmiyan decided Benin should be ruled by one of their own people, so he fathered a son with the daughter of a Benin chief, and this child became the first Oba of a new dynasty. Benin City's hey-day was in the 16th century. European travelers describe a walled city about 25 miles in circumference, neatly laid out houses with verandas, broad avenues, an ornate royal palace, and a lavish court. The Edo people were talented bronze sculptors. As with many African kingdoms, all bronzework was commissioned by and the property of the king. In a sad tale, Benin City was captured by the British in 1897, and brutally destroyed and burned. Many of the bronze sculptures were taken and are now on display in museums in London and Germany.

East of the Niger River the Ibo (Igbo) communities were scattered throughout the forest. They lived in kinship groups, each with its own leaders. The separate villages traded with one another, and occasionally waged wars, but had no central government binding them together. Social status and behavior was firmly dictated by membership in age-grades and secret societies. *Things Fall Apart* by Chinua Achebe gives a wonderful snapshot of Ibo life before the British arrived on the scene. Many Ibo people were killed in the tragic Nigerian civil war of 1966. Today, along with the Hausa and the Yoruba, they are still one of the three major ethnic groups in Nigeria.

Green Bananas with Coconut Milk and Lime

Use pure, unsweetened coconut milk to make this rich, velvety sauce. Be sure to shake the can well before opening to distribute the cream. You must use green (unripe) bananas in this recipe. You can peel them more easily if you cut through the peel lengthwise with a sharp knife and slide your fingers under the peel to pull it off. Serve this sauce over rice.

1 tablespoon butter
1 onion, chopped
1 cup (240 milliliters) coconut milk
½ teaspoon salt
1 tablespoon lime juice
1 small potato, peeled, boiled and mashed
2 green bananas, peeled and sliced into ½-inch (1½ centimeter) slices

1. Melt butter in large saucepan. Add onion and simmer until soft, about 5 minutes.
2. Add coconut milk, salt, and lime juice. Simmer over medium heat, uncovered, 5 minutes.
3. Add mashed potato and banana slices, and 2 cups (475 milliliters) of water. Bring to a boil and simmer 30 minutes over medium-low heat, stirring occasionally, until sauce has the consistency of heavy cream.

Yield: 4 servings

Breadfruit with Tomato and Peppers

Fresh breadfruit may be available in your supermarket. Buy it and use it while still green, since it begins to sour as it ripens. If fresh is not available, look for canned breadfruit in a Spanish or African food store.

1 pound (500 grams) can of breadfruit, or 1 fresh breadfruit
¼ cup (60 milliliters) peanut oil
1 onion, sliced thin
3 tomatoes, sliced thin
3 tablespoons tomato paste
½ teaspoon ground red pepper or 1 tablespoon chopped fresh hot peppers
1 green bell pepper, seeded and sliced in thin rings
½ teaspoon salt

1. If you are using fresh breadfruit, peel with a sharp knife. Cut in quarters lengthwise, and remove center core and any brown spots from the middle. Cut into 1-inch (2½ centimeter) cubes. Cover with water in a medium saucepan and bring to a boil. Simmer about 15 minutes, until breadfruit is soft. Reserve ½ cup (120 milliliters) of the cooking water, and drain. If using canned breadfruit, reserve ½ cup of the water from can, and drain breadfruit.

2. Heat the oil in a large skillet, and fry onion over medium-high heat 5 minutes. Add tomato slices and continue to simmer another 10 minutes.

3. Add tomato paste, red and green peppers, salt and liquid reserved from breadfruit. Mix well and simmer another 20 minutes, over medium heat.

4. Add breadfruit pieces and mix with sauce. Heat through. Serve with rice.

Yield: 4 servings

Variation: **Plantain with Tomato and Peppers** – Substitute 2 fresh, ripe plantains for the breadfruit. Peel plantains by cutting through the peel lengthwise with a sharp knife and sliding fingers under the peel to pull it off. Slice crosswise into 1 inch slices. Cover with water in a medium saucepan and bring to a boil. Simmer until soft, about 15 minutes. Drain liquid, reserving ½ cup. Set aside and continue with recipe as above, adding plantain in step 4.

Breadfruit with tomatoes and peppers

Fresh breadfruit

Fiery Pepper Sauce

You can use an extremely hot variety of peppers such as habaneros to make a scorching sauce, or a milder pepper to make something more edible. Much of a pepper's heat is in the seeds, so you can discard them when chopping the peppers if you would like a milder sauce. Be sure to wear rubber gloves while you are handling the peppers. You can serve this over rice, and it is especially good soaked up with fufu.

½ to 1 cup (240 milliliters) palm oil or peanut oil (add 1 teaspoon paprika to peanut oil for red colour)
6 fresh hot peppers, seeded if desired and chopped fine
4 tomatoes, chopped
2 onions, chopped
½ teaspoon salt

1. For a smoother sauce, you can grind peppers, tomatoes and onions together in a food processor or blender. If you like a chunky sauce, leave them chopped.
2. Heat oil in saucepan or skillet. Add chopped peppers, tomatoes, onions and salt. Simmer over medium heat, stirring occasionally, 20 to 30 minutes.

Yield: 4 servings

Fiery pepper sauce

Tomatoes and okra with sliced eggs

Tomatoes and Okra with Sliced Eggs

Mild egg flavour complements this perfect blend of spicy tomato and okra. Try it in place of an omelette for an African-style brunch.

½ cup (120 milliliters) peanut oil
1 onion, chopped
4 tomatoes, chopped
10 ounces (300 grams) fresh or frozen okra, stemmed and sliced crosswise
½ teaspoon salt
½ teaspoon ground red pepper
4 cups (480 grams) cooked rice
4 hardboiled eggs, peeled

1. Heat oil in skillet. Add onion, tomatoes, okra, salt and red pepper, bring to a boil, and simmer for 15 minutes over medium heat. Stir occasionally and add a small amount of water only if necessary.
2. For each serving, place 1 cup of rice on a plate. Spoon sauce over rice. Top each serving with one sliced egg.

Yield: 4 servings

Note: See photo on page 157.

Kale with Tomato and Roasted Peanuts

Peanuts, which grow abundantly throughout West Africa, give this dish a pleasing texture and crunch. You can substitute any type of fresh greens for the kale. It only takes about half an hour to prepare if you have the ingredients prepped ahead of time. Serve this delicious sauce over rice.

1 pound (500 grams) fresh greens such as kale, stemmed and chopped (8 cups)
⅓ cup (75 milliliters) plus 2 tablespoons peanut oil
1 cup whole roasted peanuts
1 onion, chopped
2 tomatoes, chopped
¼ teaspoon ground red pepper

1. Bring 1 cup (240 milliliters) water to a boil in a medium saucepan. Add kale, cover, and simmer 5 minutes until the leaves are soft. Drain, squeezing out extra water, and set aside.
2. Heat the 2 tablespoons peanut oil in a large skillet. Add peanuts and fry over medium-high heat until browned, about 5 minutes, turning frequently and watching to be sure they do not burn. Remove peanuts and drain on a paper towel. Discard remaining oil in pan and wipe it clean with a paper towel.
3. Heat the ⅓ cup peanut oil in the same large skillet. Add onion, tomatoes and red pepper and simmer 10 minutes over medium heat.
4. Add the cooked kale to the onion and tomato mixture. Combine well, and heat through.
5. Stir in peanuts just before serving.

Yield: 4 servings

Note: You can substitute 10 ounces (300 grams) frozen or 4 cups cooked kale for fresh kale.

Mushroom and Kale Sauce

I like to use kale in this spicy sauce, but you can substitute any type of dark, leafy greens. It is delicious served with rice.

2 tablespoons peanut oil
3 tablespoons tomato paste
1 onion, sliced
½ teaspoon salt
¼ teaspoon ground red pepper
2 cups (475 milliliters) broth
½ pound (250 grams) fresh whole white mushrooms
12 ounces (375 grams) fresh kale or other greens, chopped (6 to 7 cups)

1. Heat oil in a large skillet. Add tomato paste, onion, salt, red pepper and broth. Simmer over medium heat, covered, 10 minutes.
2. Slice larger mushrooms and leave the smaller ones whole. Add mushrooms and chopped greens to the skillet and stir to combine. Lower heat and simmer, covered, about 15 minutes.

Yield: 4 servings

Note: You can substitute 8 ounces (250 grams) frozen or 3 cups cooked kale for fresh kale.

Plantains with Tomato and Greens

Plantains are a wonderful substitute for meat with their sweet, yet savory taste and firm bite. You can use either ripe or green plantains for this sauce, but if you use green ones you may need to cook the sauce a bit longer before they are tender. You can mash the plantains and serve them with the sauce, or leave them in chunks and serve with rice.

3 plantains
½ cup (120 milliliters) peanut oil
1 onion, chopped
1 tomato, chopped
1 green pepper, seeded and sliced in thin rings
½ teaspoon ground red pepper
½ teaspoon salt
½ teaspoon ground ginger
1 tablespoon tomato paste
½ pound (250 grams) fresh greens such as kale or collard greens, stemmed and chopped (4 cups)

1. Peel plantains by making several slits down the length of the plantain with a sharp knife, and sliding fingers under peel to remove it. Slice into 1-inch (2½ centimeter) chunks.
2. Heat oil in large saucepan and add onion. Simmer 5 minutes over medium heat. Add tomato, green pepper, red pepper, salt, ginger and tomato paste and continue to simmer for 10 minutes.
3. Add plantains and chopped greens. Add 1½ cups (360 milliliters) water, cover and bring to a boil. Remove lid and simmer over medium heat, uncovered, until plantains are soft and sauce thickens, about 30 minutes.

Yield: 4 servings

Note: You can substitute 5 ounces (150 grams) frozen or 1 cup cooked spinach or other greens for fresh greens. You can substitute 1½ teaspoons yaji (page 187) for the ginger, red pepper and salt.

Spicy Pumpkin and Eggplant Stew

This fragrant and colourful stew, thickened with puréed vegetables, is a wonderful way to use fall pumpkins. If pumpkins are not in season just substitute a dark orange or yellow squash, such as acorn squash. Serve this stew over rice.

¼ small fresh sugar or pie pumpkin, or ½ small squash
½ small eggplant (about ½ pound/250 grams)
1 onion, half coarsely chopped and half thinly sliced
1 tomato, half coarsely chopped and half thinly sliced
1 green pepper, seeded, half coarsely chopped, and half thinly sliced
¼ cup (60 milliliters) peanut oil
1 tablespoon tomato paste
½ teaspoon coriander
½ teaspoon salt
½ teaspoon ground red pepper

1. Peel skin from pumpkin or squash with a sharp paring knife and cut into 1-inch (2½ centimeter) cubes. Set aside.
2. Peel eggplant and cut into 1-inch (2½ centimeter) cubes. Set aside.
3. Grind the coarsely chopped onion, tomato and green pepper in food processor or blender until smooth.
4. Heat oil in a large, heavy pot. Add ground vegetables and simmer over medium heat 5 minutes.
5. Add sliced onion, tomato and green pepper, tomato paste, coriander, salt and red pepper to pot. Continue to simmer for 10 minutes.
6. Stir in pumpkin cubes and 1 cup (240 milliliters) of water. Cover and cook over medium heat for 10 minutes.
7. Add eggplant to pot. Cover, lower heat and simmer 20 minutes more, checking and adding more water if it becomes too thick.

Yield: 4 servings

White Bean, Spinach and Groundnut Sauce

Peanut butter thickens this simple sauce and blends well with the spicy flavours. You can serve it with rice, fufu or tuwo.

½ cup (100 grams) dry, white beans or black-eyed peas, soaked overnight, or 1½ cups cooked beans
2 tablespoons peanut oil or palm oil
1 small onion, chopped
½ teaspoon ground red pepper
½ teaspoon salt
½ teaspoon ginger
1 tablespoon tomato paste
2 cups (475 milliliters) broth
½ pound (250 grams) fresh spinach, stemmed and chopped (4 cups)
1 tablespoon smooth, unsweetened peanut butter

1. If you are using dry beans, cover with water in a saucepan and bring to a boil. Simmer until tender, about 1 hour. Drain and set aside.
2. Heat oil in a large skillet or stir fry pan. Add onion and cook over medium-high heat for 5 minutes.
3. Add red pepper, salt, ginger and tomato paste to skillet. Mix well and continue to simmer.
4. Add beans, 1½ cups broth and spinach to skillet. Cover and cook 5 minutes until spinach is wilted.
5. Mix peanut butter with remaining ½ cup broth. Add this mixture to skillet and combine well.
6. Bring mixture to a boil and simmer over medium heat just until thickened about 10 minutes.

Yield: 4 servings

Note: You can substitute 5 ounces (150 grams) frozen or 1 cup cooked spinach for fresh spinach. You can substitute 1½ tsp yaji (page 187) for the red pepper, salt and ginger.

The Mossi

Hundreds of years ago the Upper Volta River valley (in Burkina Faso today) was populated by many small, independent groups without any central government. Around the 14th century local legends say a band of men came from the east across the Niger River, travelling on horseback. These newcomers united the people, bringing the Mossi states into existence. At this time the Mossi were an aggressive people, raiding the savannah right up to the edges of the Sahara, and even sacking Timbuktu. It was Sunni Ali Ber, the Songhai ruler, who finally drove them back to the Upper Volta River valley, where they have remained peacefully to this day.

Throughout the centuries the Mossi have preserved their traditional religions. Although the rulers had political power, everyone understood that the priests held the prosperity of the nation in their hands. This was probably easier because the area did not produce many valuable trade items such as the gold or kola nuts abundant in other parts of West Africa. Since Muslim traders were never attracted to the area in great numbers, Islam did not have the influence here that it did in the rest of West Africa.

Today the Mossi live in Burkina Faso and Ivory Coast, along the Black and White Volta River valleys and plains.

Garaje ga dami ya che a zuba miya
Haste sees a bundle of corn and says let the sauce be poured on.

Desserts

Paw-paw mango fool

A light sorbet or tropical fruit salad can refresh you after a satisfying West African dinner. If you have a sweet tooth, there is something here for you as well. A traditional West African meal does not include dessert, and many of these recipes are influenced by the French and British colonials in West Africa.

Contents

The Tuareg: Blue Men of the Desert

Warriors have swept down from the desert upon West Africa for thousands of years, often creating the weakness which caused an empire to crumble. The Tuareg of today are nomadic desert dwellers, descended from those fierce North African Berbers. They ride their camels into northern cities of the West African Sahel, still carrying on the ancient salt trade. Armed with swords, their faces veiled, they look mysterious and warlike. They are often employed as guards in the cities when they move south during the dry season. They will set up camp in front of the building they have been hired to watch, cooking over an open fire and brewing tea in a large metal teapot.

The indigo blue dye on the robes of the nobility sometimes rubs off on their skin, hence the nickname, "blue men of the desert." The warrior class wear white robes and veils. Tuaregs depend on their camels for desert travel and regard them as highly as we would a household pet, naming them and even writing songs about them.

Tuareg women enjoy much freedom and equality in their society. They can own property, choose their own husbands, and then divorce them if they please. In a reversal of Muslim tradition, the women walk about with their faces uncovered while the men are heavily veiled.

Kamshin arziki ya fi kamshi waina.
The scent of generosity is better than the scent of cakes.

Guava Sorbet with Lime

This sweet and aromatic sorbet will cool you down after a spicy African meal. You can make it in a food processor, or you can complete steps 1 and 2, then transfer to an ice cream freezer and freeze according to manufacturer's directions.

1½ cups (375 milliliters) guava nectar (12-ounce can)
½ cup (120 milliliters) simple syrup (recipe below)
1 tablespoon lime juice
lime to slice for garnish

1. In a large bowl, mix guava nectar, 1 cup (240 milliliters) water, simple syrup and lime juice.
2. Pour into a shallow metal 9x13 inch baking pan, cover with foil and place in freezer for 2 hours. It should freeze to an icy slush. If it is still liquid, return to freezer for another half hour.
3. Break mixture up into chunks and transfer to food processor. Purée until smooth. Meanwhile, place an airtight plastic container into the freezer to chill.
4. Transfer slush to chilled container and return to freezer for at least 20 minutes. Before serving, thaw in refrigerator for 10 minutes, longer if it has frozen solid. Scoop into a dessert glass or fancy bowl and serve garnished with lime.

Yield: 3 cups sorbet

Simple Syrup

This makes more than enough for the guava sorbet. You can use leftovers to make lemonade.

2 cups (400 grams) sugar
1 cup (250 milliliters) water

1. Combine sugar and water in a small saucepan and bring to a boil. Simmer 1 minute, until mixture is clear and sugar is dissolved.

Guava sorbet with lime

Coconut cream

Coconut Cream

Coconut flavour adds a new dimension to this classic cream dessert. Prepare in small individual molds garnished with flowers and papaya purée.

2½ **cups (600 milliliters) unsweetened coconut milk, shaken well before opening**
1 **cup (200 grams) sugar**
2 **envelopes unflavoured gelatin**
2 **cups sour cream**
1 **teaspoon vanilla**

1. Combine coconut milk, sugar and gelatin in a small saucepan and cook over low-medium heat just until sugar and gelatin are dissolved. Remove from heat.
2. Stir in sour cream and vanilla, beating until smooth. Pour into 6 individual dessert molds.
3. Chill at least 3 hours. Remove from molds by placing in warm water for a few seconds.

Yield: 6 individual desserts

Note: To make papaya purée for garnish, peel a whole papaya, remove seeds, and cut in large chunks. Purée in food processor or blender until smooth. Stir in 1 tablespoon lime juice.

Note: See photo on page 169.

Baked Green Bananas in Orange Syrup

This is a sweet way to use up a surplus of green (unripe) bananas. After you prepare this dish you will want to serve it right away since the bananas begin to turn brown as they sit.

½ cup (120 milliliters) orange juice
½ cup (100 grams) sugar
2 bananas
3 tablespoons lemon juice

1. Preheat oven to 350°F (175°C).
2. Combine orange juice and sugar in small saucepan and bring to a boil. Simmer uncovered 5 minutes.
3. Peel bananas and cut in half lengthwise, as you would for a banana split, then crosswise, to make 4 pieces. Place in oven proof dish, with cut sides up. Brush lemon juice over tops of bananas.
4. Pour syrup over bananas. Bake 10 minutes, uncovered.
5. To serve, place two banana pieces in each small serving bowl, and spoon syrup over top. Serve immediately.

Yield: 4 servings

Cinnamon-Orange Chin-chin

Chin-chin is a classic West African fried pastry. The flavours of cinnamon and orange add a new twist to this recipe.

2 cups (275 grams) white, all purpose flour
½ teaspoon baking powder
½ teaspoon cinnamon
1 tablespoon grated orange peel
¼ teaspoon salt
½ cup (120 grams) butter or margarine (1 stick)
½ cup (100 grams) sugar
2 eggs
4 cups (1 liter) peanut or vegetable oil for frying

1. Combine flour, baking powder, cinnamon, orange peel and salt in a medium-sized bowl.
2. In a separate bowl cream butter and sugar together until fluffy. Add eggs one at a time, mixing well.
3. Stir dry ingredients into flour mixture. Turn out onto floured surface and knead lightly into a ball. Wrap in plastic and refrigerate at least 30 minutes.
4. Roll dough out to ⅛-inch thick. Square off ends and cut strips 7 x 1½ inches (18 x 4 centimeters). Cut a 1-inch (2½ centimeter) slit near the bottom of each strip, and pull top end down and through hole gently, making a loop. (See photo opposite) Reroll remaining dough and repeat process until all of dough is used.
5. Heat oil in a large, heavy pan to 360°F (180°C). Fry twists in batches of five, about four minutes per batch, or until golden brown. Turn once during frying. Remove from oil and drain on paper towels. Sprinkle with powdered sugar.

Yield: About 2 dozen chin-chin

Chin-chin

Chin-chin twists shaped and ready to fry

Tropical Fruit Fritters with Butterscotch Sauce

Fresh pineapple makes especially juicy fritters, or you can try your favorite tropical fruit. They are luscious dipped in creamy butterscotch sauce (recipe on opposite page).

1 egg
⅓ cup (75 milliliters) milk
1 teaspoon lime juice
½ cup (75 grams) white, all purpose flour
¼ teaspoon salt
1 tablespoon sugar
pinch of salt
3 cups fresh tropical fruits, such as pineapple, pawpaw, banana or mango, peeled and cubed
4 cups (1 liter) vegetable oil for frying

1. Separate egg white from yolk. Reserve white, and combine yolk in a medium sized bowl with the milk, lime juice, flour, ¼ teaspoon salt, and sugar. Whisk mixture together until it is free of lumps.
2. Beat egg white and pinch of salt until it forms stiff peaks. Fold into batter gently.
3. Heat oil in a large heavy pan to 360°F (180°C). Dip each fruit chunk into batter, allowing excess to drip off, and then drop into hot oil. Fry until golden brown on all sides. Continue to fry fritters in batches, draining on paper towels. Serve while still warm.

Yield: About 4 cups fritters

Butterscotch Sauce

This classic sauce is a perfect complement for tropical fruit fritters.

1 cup (225 grams) brown sugar
¼ cup (60 milliliters) light corn syrup
¼ cup (60 grams) butter (½ stick)
⅛ teaspoon salt
½ cup (120 milliliters) heavy cream
1½ teaspoon vanilla
¼ teaspoon lemon juice

1. Combine brown sugar, corn syrup, butter and salt in a medium saucepan. Bring to a boil, and boil on medium-high heat 5 minutes without stirring. Remove from heat.
2. Stir cream, vanilla and lemon juice into sugar mixture and beat well with a spoon until smooth. Transfer to serving or storage container and cool. The mixture thickens as it cools. Refrigerate leftovers.

Yield: 1½ cups

Crispy Millet Cookies

These crunchy fried cookies are a more sophisticated version of the fried dough found all over the world. The slightly bitter taste of millet gives a perfect contrast to the buttery crunch and powdered sugar coating. Be sure to leave at least 2 hours for these to sit at room temperature before frying.

1 cup (100 grams) millet flour
2 tablespoons butter
1 cup (240 milliliters) vegetable oil, for frying
powdered sugar for dipping

1. Measure millet flour into a heat-proof medium bowl.
2. Combine butter with ¾ cup (180 milliliters) water in a medium sized saucepan. Cook uncovered on medium heat until butter is melted and mixture just comes to a boil. Pour water over millet. Leave at room temperature, covered, for at least 2 hours.
3. Heat oil in a large skillet, to 360°F (180°C). Stir batter and drop by large spoonfuls into hot oil, a few at a time. Batter will spread like a pancake. If batter does not spread, thin it out with 1 or 2 tablespoons of water. Fry until golden brown, turning once. Remove from oil with a slotted spoon and drain on paper towels. Continue to fry in batches until all of batter is used. Serve with powdered sugar for dipping.

Yield: About 12 cookies

Note: You can find millet flour in health food stores and through mail order (see Sources).

Crispy millet cookies served with fresh pineapple

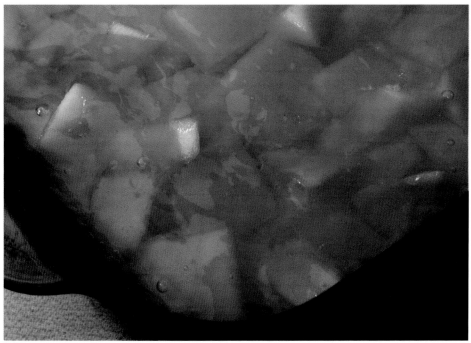

Mango custard pastry

Mango Custard Pastry

Gleaming orange jello makes this creamy dessert eye-catching. Use the recipe for stirred custard in this section, or use a commercial mix if you prefer.

Pastry ingredients:

1 cup (140 grams) white, all purpose flour
2 tablespoons sugar
½ teaspoon salt
6 tablespoons (90 grams) cold butter (¾ stick)
1 egg yolk
1 tablespoon lemon juice

Filling ingredients:

1⅔ cup stirred custard (recipe on following page)
2 large, ripe mangoes (2 to 3 cups fruit)
1 (3-ounce) packet orange gelatin
½ teaspoon vanilla extract

1. Prepare custard and set aside to cool.
2. Preheat oven to 400°F (200°C).
3. For pastry, combine flour, sugar and salt in a large mixing bowl. With a pastry blender, cut in the cold butter until it is the size of small peas. Make a well in center of mixture. Whisk together egg yolk and lemon juice in a small bowl and pour into the well. Mix liquids with the flour using a fork and then your hands until fully combined. Press mixture into the bottom of a greased or non-stick 8 x 8 pan.
4. Bake 15 minutes, or until lightly golden brown on top. Remove from oven, place pan on a rack and cool to room temperature. Do not remove pastry from pan.
5. Meanwhile, cut a thick slice from each side of mango as close to the seed as possible. Score fruit on each slice without cutting through skin. Press inward on skin to turn slice inside out, making scored pieces of fruit stand out. Slice pieces of fruit from skin. (See photo on page 97.) Slice fruit from around seed. Cut into small cubes. Repeat with second mango.
6. Dissolve the jello in 1 cup (250 milliliters) boiling water. Stir in ½ cup cold water. Set aside to cool at room temperature for 30 to 45 minutes. Do not let it set completely. It should be thick and honey-like.
7. Stir vanilla into the custard, and spread over cooled pastry.
8. Spoon diced mango pieces evenly over custard.
9. Spoon jello over mangoes and refrigerate until set, about 1 hour. Cut in squares to serve.

Yield: one (8 x 8) baking pan

Note: See photo on page 177.

Stirred Custard

This creamy custard can be used in several of the recipes in this book, or served with fresh fruit as a light dessert.

1½ cups (360 milliliters) milk
2 eggs
⅓ cup (75 grams) sugar

1. Heat milk slowly over low heat in medium saucepan until bubbles form along edges.
2. Whisk eggs and sugar together in a medium mixing bowl.
3. Pour about ½ cup of hot milk into egg mixture, whisking vigorously. Pour all of egg mixture into hot milk, stirring.
4. Cook milk mixture over medium heat, stirring, until it begins to thicken and boil.
5. Remove milk from heat, pour into bowl and press a sheet of plastic wrap over top. Cool to room temperature, stirring occasionally.

Yield: 1⅔ cups (400 milliliters)

Paw-paw Mango Fool

Britain and France introduced many of their popular foods to West Africa during colonization. The fool, a custard combined with fruit purée, is a traditional Scottish dessert often made with raspberries or blackberries. The tart flavours of tropical fruits are a natural to offset the mild custard, and make a cool, refreshing dish for a scorching climate.

1²⁄₃ cups (400 milliliters) or one recipe stirred custard (recipe page 179)
1 ripe papaya (paw-paw)
1 ripe mango
1 tablespoon lime juice

1. Prepare stirred custard according to recipe on preceding page and cool to room temperature.
2. Peel papaya, scoop out seeds from center and cut in chunks. Purée in blender or food processor. Stir lime juice into papaya purée, and set aside.
3. Cut a thick slice from each side of mango as close to the seed as possible. Score fruit on each slice with a sharp knife without cutting through skin. Press inward on skin to turn slice inside out, making scored pieces of fruit stand out. Slice pieces of fruit from skin. (See photo on page 97.) Slice remaining fruit from around seed and remove skin. Purée fruit in blender or food processor, and set aside.
4. Layer custard, mango purée and papaya purée in individual dessert glasses. Sometimes the fruit purée is stirred directly into the custard. You can chill the fool for up to an hour before serving.

Yield: 4 servings

Note: See photo on page 165.

Banana Fritters

When you want a more substantial dessert try these soft, doughnut-like fritters. Dip them in powdered sugar to complement the sweet banana flavour.

¾ cup (100 grams) white, all purpose flour
3 tablespoons sugar
2 eggs
½ cup (120 milliliters) milk
2 very ripe bananas
4 cups (1 liter) vegetable or peanut oil for frying
powdered sugar for dipping

1. Combine flour and sugar together in a large bowl. Beat eggs and milk together in a separate bowl and stir into the dry ingredients, mixing until batter is smooth.
2. Peel bananas and cut into chunks. Purée bananas in food processor or blender, or mash with a fork.
3. Add banana purée to batter and stir well.
4. Heat oil in a large, heavy pot until it reaches 375°F (190°C). Scoop ¼ cup (60 milliliters) batter and drop it into the hot oil. The batter will spread out into a flat disk. Fry only three or four fritters at a time to give them room to spread.
5. Fry fritters until golden brown, about 5 minutes. Turn once during frying. Remove with slotted spoon and drain on paper towels. Sprinkle with powdered sugar and serve warm.

Yield: 12 fritters

Pineapple Pie

Sweeten up a coffee-break or end your meal in a rich way with this Liberian specialty. You can serve it warm or at room temperature, but it is even better chilled.

1 large, ripe pineapple
pastry for 2 pie crusts
2 eggs
1 cup (200 grams) sugar
1 tablespoon lemon or lime juice
1 tablespoon butter, cut in small pieces

1. Remove top from pineapple by twisting and pulling it off. With a sharp knife cut pineapple into quarters. Slice peel from each quarter and slice off core. Grate pineapple. You should have about 3 cups.
2. Roll out one pastry crust and place in a 9-inch pie plate.
3. Beat the eggs together in a large bowl. Add sugar and lemon or lime juice and mix well.
4. Stir pineapple into the egg mixture. Pour into pie shell.
5. Dot the top of the pineapple mixture with butter. Moisten outside edges of pie shell, and lay the top pastry over filling, pressing edges together to seal.
6. Flute edges or press with tines of fork to make a pattern. Cut several slits in the top of the pie for air to escape.
7. Bake pie at 425°F (220°C) for 10 minutes. Reduce heat to 350°F (175°C) and bake for another 35 minutes, until crust is browned.

Yield: One (9-inch) pie

Fried Plantains with Sugar and Cream

Sweet plantains with the caramel flavours of brown sugar and cream are a mild way to end your meal. This recipe can easily be increased for a larger group. The amount of oil used for frying will remain the same.

1 ripe plantain (completely yellow with black spots)
1 cup (240 milliliters) vegetable oil
½ cup (120 milliliters) light cream (more or less as desired)
2 tablespoons brown sugar

1. Peel plantains by cutting through peel with a sharp knife the length of the plantain, then sliding fingers under peel to remove.
2. Slice plantains in half lengthwise as you would for a banana split, and then cut crosswise in half to make four pieces. Heat oil in a heavy skillet over medium-high heat for about 5 minutes, until a small piece of plantain dropped in begins to sizzle. Fry plantain slices until golden on each side. Remove and drain on paper towels.
3. Place two plantain slices in each small bowl. Drizzle with cream as desired, and sprinkle each with one tablespoon brown sugar. Serve immediately.

Yield: 2 servings

Tropical Fruit Salad

A tropical fruit salad is a refreshing and natural end to an African meal. Even in New England there is a colourful spectrum of fresh tropical fruits to choose from. Feel free to experiment with the types of fruit available in your area. Some fresh, toasted coconut flakes and ruby-red pomegranate seeds are all you need to dress this salad up.

1 papaya	**1 banana**
1 avocado	**1 orange**
1 mango	**pomegranate seeds**
2 to 3 guavas	**toasted coconut flakes**
1 fresh pineapple	

1. Cut papaya in half lengthwise, and scoop seeds from inside. Discard seeds, peel and cut fruit into 1-inch (2½ centimeter) cubes.
2. Slice through avocado lengthwise all the way through to the seed. Twist and pull the two halves away from the seed. Dig tip of knife into seed and pull it out of fruit. Peel and cut into 1-inch cubes.
3. Cut 1 thick slice from each side of mango, cutting as far in toward the seed as possible. On each slice, score through the fruit with a sharp knife until you reach the skin. Do not cut through skin. With both hands, push skin out so that the cubes of fruit stand out from it. (See photo on page 97.) Slice cubes from skin. Slice fruit from around the seed.
4. Peel guavas, cut in half and remove seeds with tip of sharp knife. Cut into chunks.
5. Twist leafy top from pineapple. Slice fruit down the middle, lengthwise, with a large, sharp knife. Slice each half down the middle lengthwise again. Slice off tough core from center of each quarter. Slice off peel, and "eyes". Dice fruit into 1-inch cubes.
6. Peel banana and slice into rounds. Toss with lemon juice if not serving immediately, to keep them from turning brown.
7. Peel orange and divide into sections.
8. Mix all fruit together in a large bowl. Sprinkle with toasted coconut flakes and pomegranate seeds.

Yield: 6 servings

Tropical fruit salad garnished with toasted coconut and pomegranate seeds.

Da in chi dadi in yi wahala gara in chi mara dadi a fuche.
Rather than eat that which is sweet and have trouble, would I eat that
which lacks sweetness in peace.

A selection of hot peppers.

Burning Decisions: How to Select Hot Peppers

Capsaicin, the chemical that gives hot peppers their heat, is concentrated in the veins of the pepper, and to a lesser extent in the skin and seeds. In 1912, Wilbur Scoville developed a method of measuring this heat. It is a subjective rating, based on taste tests, which measures the amount of sugar water that needs to be added to a hot pepper solution before the heat from the peppers is masked. This scale is still used today to compare the strength of different varieties of peppers. The numbers are always given in a range, and sources often disagree, since even one type of pepper can be hotter or milder depending on the conditions under which its grown. However, the Scoville scale is useful for grouping peppers into categories of mild, medium hot, hot and extremely hot. The chart below gives Scoville Units for some commonly found peppers.

Dangerously Hot Peppers
Habanero and Scotch Bonnet   100,000 to 300,000
African Bird   100,000 to 130,000

Very Hot Peppers
Thai, Piquin and Chiltepin   50,000 to 100,000
Cayenne,Tabasco and Aji   30,000 to 50,000

Medium Hot Peppers
Serrano and Guajillo   5000 to 15,000
Jalapeno   3500 to 5000

Mild Peppers
Poblano and Pasilla   2500 to 3000
Ancho and Anaheim   1000 to 1500
New Mexico   500 to 1000

Child's Play Peppers
Cherry peppers   100 to 500
Bell and Cubanelle   0 to 100

Yaji is a Hausa word for a mixture of spices and hot pepper. The recipe sometimes includes up to seven different spices. A simple version you can put together no matter where you live is equal amounts of ground red pepper, ground ginger and salt. If you keep some yaji on hand you can throw it into many dishes for a bit of spice and bite. The name Yaji dates back to 14th century Kano. The ruler at that time was nicknamed Yaji, or "hot-tempered one".

Chili powder is a mixture of several spices, and should not be substituted for ground red peppers in these recipes.

Be sure to wear rubber gloves when handling very hot peppers, since the capsaicin is easily transferred to your skin and eyes, and will burn painfully.

photo by Thadd Jackson

Red peppers for sale in the Lagos market

Komai ya yi zafi, ya yi sauki.
Everything that gets hot will cool down.

Sources of West African Foods

In major cities throughout the northern hemisphere there is usually a grocer supplying traditional foods to any West African population. It may be a large grocery chain that carries ethnic foods, or just a tiny Spanish or Oriental market with a shelf of African products. If you poke around and find out where people shop, you will be surprised at what you find.

You can purchase many of the foods you will need through the following mail order sources:

Adriana's Caravan
409 Vanderbilt Street
Brooklyn, NY 11218
(800) 316-0820   adricara@aol.com
Palm oil, ground crayfish, red pepper, and more. She carries just about every spice on earth!

Calabash
45 Edison Place
Newark, NJ 07102
(973) 643-7828
You can get just about any West African foods here, including daddawa! Call for availability.

Frieda's By Mail
4465 Corporate Center Drive
Los Alamitos, CA 90720-2561
(800) 241-1771   mailorder@friedas.com
http://www.friedas.com
Frieda's carries exotic fruits and vegetables.

Kitchen Market
218 Eighth Avenue at 21st St.
New York, NY 10011
(888) 468-4433
You can buy dried tropical fruits and whole dried shrimp from this catalog.

The Bakers Catalog
PO Box 876
Norwich, Vermont 05055-0876
(800) 827-6836   http://www.kingarthurflour.com
Try this catalog for rice and millet flour, unsweetened coconut flakes and potato starch.

The Oriental Pantry
423 Great Road
Acton, MA 01720 oriental@orientalpantry.com
(800) 828-0368   http://www.orientalpantry.com
Coconut milk, shrimp paste, maggi sauce, dried shrimp, rice flour and cookware are available.

Rafal Spice Company
2521 Russell
Detroit, Michigan 48207
(313) 259-6373
Order kola nuts, plantain leaves, potato starch, angostura bitters, maggi sauce or marmite here.

African Home Supply, Ltd
http://www.afrifood.com
(800) 993-9801
This company based in Chicago sells many, many African foods. Check their online catalog.

These African food distributors may be able to tell you of grocers in your area who sell their products:

Sands African Imports, Ltd.
923 Frelinghuysen Ave.
Newark NJ 07114
(973) 824-5500

Prince and Brothers
(413) 739-7214
fax-(413) 739-9368

Makola African Market Imports
375 Lyons Ave.
Newark, NJ 07112
(973) 926-3919 (mailorder, call for price list)

Nina International
PO Box 6566
Hyattsville, MD 20789

Fulani woman with kola nuts

Sa zuchiya ga chi, shi ya kawo jin yunwa.
It is setting the heart on eating that brings on hunger.

Glossary of Tropical Foods

Foods which are not readily available outside the tropics are not called for in these recipes, yet many still merit a description for those who remember them or are lucky enough to be able to find them.

Fruits

Avocado: *(Persia gratissima)* This fruit is about the size and shape of a pear, and often called avocado pear. The dark green skin, which can be bumpy or smooth, covers a soft, light green, buttery flesh. A hard, oval pit is in the center.

Baobab: *(Adansonia digitata)* The dried, powdered leaves of this enormous tree, which the Hausa call kuka, are added to soups and stews to give them a slippery texture similar to okra. The fruit of the tree is a large oval, 10 to 12 inches long. It is downy on the outside, with a woody shell covering compartments filled with fibrous pulp. It is sometimes called monkey bread. Powdered baobab may be found in African food stores or by mail order. (See photo on page 9.)

Breadfruit: *(Artocarpus communis)* This round, bright green fruit grows on a large tree. It is about 8 inches in diameter, seedless, and covered with a thick rind. After ripening fully, it develops a sour taste, so it should be used before it becomes soft. Breadfruit has a mealy texture and can be eaten raw, in a sauce, or simply peeled, boiled and served with a butter sauce. Breadfruit is sometimes available fresh in groceries, or can be purchased canned. (See photo on page 155.) It should not be confused with jackfruit, which is much larger, oblong, and contains large seeds.

Cashew Fruit: *(Anacardium occidentale)* Cashew fruit grows on a large, spreading tree. One cashew nut hangs from the bottom of each fruit. The 3-inch fruit is either yellow or rosy red. It is deliciously sour enough to make your whole mouth pucker. (See photo on page 13.)

Cizaki: *(Carissa edulis)* These small, dark red berries have 4 to 5 hard seeds, and a sticky white latex juice. They can be used for jellies and jams, or puréed and mixed in a fool.

Coconut: *(Cocos nucifera)* The fruit of the coconut palm have a greenish-brown outer husk 2 to 3 inches thick covering a brown hairy nut. Under this is a thin brown membrane covering the white meat. Inside the meat is the *coconut water*. You can drink the water, or use it to make a delicious rice. The meat is edible and often grated for cooking. *Coconut milk* is made by pouring boiling water over the grated meat to render the oil, then squeezing oil from pulp to get a rich, white liquid. Today it is easy to buy canned coconut milk. Be sure to get unsweetened, and shake the can before opening it to disperse the cream. Sometimes you can find young, unhusked coconuts for sale. The husk can be sliced off with a sharp knife. Inside, the nut will be creamy coloured and fibrous, but will not have the brown, hairy covering yet. Crack the nut with a hammer to get at the water and meat. The meat will be thinner, and soft enough to scoop out of shell with a spoon. There is more water in a young coconut. See page 62 for method to shell a mature coconut.

Guava: *(Psidium guajava)* This round fruit ranges from 1 to 4 inches in diameter. A thin green or yellow skin covers the soft and fragrant pinkish fruit with many tiny seeds in the center. Guavas do not keep very well and the fresh fruit is only available in warmer climates. Northerners can buy guava nectar, guava jelly, and dried guava slices.

Mango: *(Mangifera indica)* The large leafy mango tree is a common sight in West Africa, with smooth, heavy fruit which falls to the ground upon ripening. Mangoes start out green and hard, turning softer and rosy as they mature. Peel before eating, and slice the fruit away from the large, flat white pit in the center. The yellow fruit will taste sweeter if it is allowed to ripen fully. This fruit is easy to find in the produce section of most supermarkets. (See photo on page 97.)

Papaya: *(Carica papaya)* Also known as paw-paw, this fruit, which comes in a range of sizes, is rounded on one end and tapering on the other. The green skin will turn yellow as it ripens. The peach or pink coloured fruit has a small circle of round, dark seeds in the center, which should be removed. Paw-paw makes a very pretty fruit salad or purée for a pudding or garnish. You can usually find it in the produce section of your supermarket.

Pitanga Cherry: *(Eugenia uniflora)* This juicy red fruit with a very unique taste grows on a large decorative shrub. The cherries are ½ to 1 inch in diameter, and ribbed from top to bottom. They are also called Surinam cherries or Brazilian cherries. Pitanga cherries make excellent jelly. They are not usually available outside the tropics.

Plantain: *(Musa fehi)* Originally from Asia, the plantain looks like a large green banana, which turns yellow and then black as it ripens. This fruit should not be eaten raw, but can be fried, roasted, broiled, boiled, mashed or grilled.

Pomegranate: *(Punica granatum)* This round, reddish-brown fruit is about the size of an orange, with a thick, leathery rind. Break open the outer skin and you will find many compartments filled with small, red juicy seeds. You can nudge these out with your fingers and eat them. Or use a spoon, to avoid turning your hands purple. The seeds freeze well, and make a striking garnish. Many supermarkets carry pomegranates in their produce section when they are in season.

Grains

Cornmeal: Maize was imported from the Americas in the 16th century. Today it is used in many fried snack foods, or fermented to make kenkey and banku – thick starches served with a spicy sauce. Yellow cornmeal works well in these recipes.

Millet: Several varieties of millet have been grown in West Africa for centuries. This nutty and slightly bitter grain is made into tuwo or used for a large variety of fried and boiled snacks. It is also known as gero or acha. Millet is available in health food stores, or see Sources for mail order.

Rice Flour: Rice is grown in many of the wet coastal areas and around the river valleys of West Africa. Ground rice, or rice flour, is used to make snacks, breads and fufu. You can buy rice flour in health food stores, or grind your own from whole rice. Many sauces can be served with boiled rice.

Sorghum: This staple grain has been grown for hundreds of years in West Africa, but is hard to find in northern countries except as animal feed. Sorghum makes a delicious porridge which the Hausa call kunu. The British referred to sorghum as Kafir corn, and many old West African cookbooks will call for corn when they mean sorghum.   It is also called guinea corn, or dawa.

Vegetables

Cassava: *(Manihot utilissima)* This waxy tuber, also called manioc and yuca, was brought from the Americas in the 16th century. Tapioca is made from cassava. The raw roots contain hydrocyanic acid, which can be toxic until it is cooked or dried in the sun. The flesh underneath the bark-like peel is white and hard, and can be cut in chunks and boiled or added to stews. Cassava leaves are added to stews and can be purchased dried or canned in African food stores. Fresh cassava is easily found in the produce section of many supermarkets.

Cocoyam: *(Colocasia esculenta)* While men are in charge of farming the true yam, women tend to the smaller cocoyam gardens. This root was imported from Asia around 1000 A.D. It is a West African variety of the taro or dasheen which is used to make Poi in the South Pacific.

Garden Eggs: These cream coloured vegetables are the size and shape of an egg. You may be able to find them canned in northern climates. They can be used in place of eggplant.

Gari: Cassava is ground, fermented and roasted to make this coarse flour. Gari has a slightly sour taste which complements breads or fufu, or the popular dish called gari foto. It is available in most African food stores. (See photo on page 83.)

Greens: There are dozens of varieties of dark, leafy greens used in West Africa. One of the most common is bitterleaf, which must be washed thoroughly before cooking to remove the bitter taste. Cassava leaves, ewedu, red sorrel or yakuwa, lansur (a parsley-like leaf vegetable) and pumpkin leaves are also common.   Dried bitterleaf is sold in African food stores. No matter what type of climate you live in you will find many substitutions, including spinach, kale, beet greens, swiss chard, dandelion, turnip greens, or collards. Do not substitute lettuce for dark leafy greens.

Hot Pepper: *(Capsicum frutescens)* Many different types, colours and sizes of hot peppers are available in West Africa, but the one thing they have in common is heat.   If you like spicy food, do not hold back here. The Africans use peppers generously to make what can only be described as fiery dishes.   Remove the veins and seeds to decrease the heat. The amounts called for in these recipes are middle of the road. If you are a novice at hot foods you may want to decrease the pepper a bit. If you grew up eating searing tuwo da miya, you will want to add a bit more pepper than the recipe calls for. See page 186 for more information. For ground red pepper, use an African brand if you can find it.

Okra: *(Hibiscus sabdariffa)* These pointed, ridged green pods have a stem on one end, and many small round whitish seeds inside. They give sauces a slippery texture very common in African foods. The more you chop them and release the seeds, the more thickening power they will have. Ground okra powder will make a sauce downright gelatinous, so use it sparingly. Okra pods become fibrous as they grow so the smaller ones – about 3 inches long – are preferable for cooking. They are available canned, fresh or frozen.

Melons and Gourds: *(Cucurbita)* Pumpkin, called *ponkie* in Nigeria, is boiled, mashed, fried or used in sauces and rice. Calabashes are large baskets made of hollowed gourds.

Sugar Cane: *(Saccharum officinarum)* These bamboo-like stalks are sugary sweet, and chewing them is a pleasant pastime. See Sources for sugar cane swizzlers.

Yams: *(Dioscorea rotundata)* This king of African crops has been cultivated in West Africa for thousands of years. Yams have been known to reach one hundred pounds, and grow to eight feet long. In many societies a man's very worth is determined by the size of his yam harvest. The closest yam in American markets is *name (nah-may)*, which is often imported from Costa Rica. It has a dark brown bark-like skin and cream-coloured flesh underneath. Real African yams, often imported from Ghana, are an even better choice. In a Spanish grocery they will be labeled *name africanos*. There are many other varieties of yam-like tubers for sale.

Seeds and Beans

Agbono: This ground seed is used for its thickening properties. Like okra and baobab, it gives a sauce the popular slippery texture.

Black-eyed Peas: *(Vigna unguiculata)* These legumes, also called cowpeas, are a staple of West African cooking and are used in just about every type of dish from stews to starches to snacks like kosai and moyin-moyin. African slaves transported black-eyed peas to America, and they still play a prominent part in Southern American cooking. Many people eat a dish with black-eyed peas on New Years day to bring good luck in the coming year.

Daddawa: This black, fermented paste is made from the flat beans of the locust tree, *Parkia fili-coidea*. This is a different tree from the European locust tree, which produces carob beans. Daddawa, also known as iru or ogili, is stored in hard cakes. It is extremely smelly, but adds a wonderful flavour to sauces. Daddawa is sold in cakes, balls or bouillon cubes, only from specialized West African grocers. Maggi Sauce can be substituted.

Egusi: These ground melon seeds are used to thicken stews and as part of a steamed dumpling. Egusi is available either whole or ground in African food stores. (See photo on page 127.)

Kola Nuts: These brownish-orange, bitter nuts about the size of a chestnut grow in pods on a tree *(cola nitida)* in the wet coastal forests. Many West Africans enjoy chewing them, and claim they give an extra burst of energy. In social rituals a guest is always welcomed with a kola nut, just as many Westerners welcome visitors with a cup of coffee. In fact, kola nuts contain 2 to 3 times the caffeine of coffee beans, and are also known as Soudan Coffee. Its easy to spot a kola nut connoisseur by his orange teeth. See Sources for mail order catalogs which carry them. (See photo on page 189.)

Peanuts: *(Arachis hypogaea)* These legumes are well suited to the West African climate and are a staple food as well as a cash crop. They are known by the English name of groundnuts. In Kano peanuts used to be stacked in gigantic pyramids ready to be shipped off for export. They were also ground and pressed into oil in the factories there, filling the streets of the city with the smell of the fresh, roasted nuts. Peanut butter is used as a thickener in many dishes such as groundnut chop.

Fish

Fish can be categorized as fat or lean to help determine the best types to use in a particular recipe. Many of the varieties below are available in West Africa, with its broad coastline and several large rivers. Shellfish such as shrimp, crayfish, crabs and lobster are also popular.

Fat Fish: Fat fish can tolerate dryer cooking methods such as broiling or baking. They do not take too well to deep frying or excessive oil. Fat fish often have a strong flavour and are well suited to the spicy sauces of West African cooking. Bluefish, mackerel, salmon, shark, swordfish, tuna, trout, whitefish, butterfish, shad, herring and some catfish are among the fat fish.

Lean Fish: Lean fish are low in fat, and can become very dry if they are not cooked properly or are overcooked. They should be cooked by moist heat methods, such as poaching or cooking in a soup or stew, or fried. If you broil or bake a lean fish be sure to baste with butter, oil, or a liquid to prevent drying. Some lean fish are flounder, sole, halibut, turbot, cod, haddock, perch, grouper, pike and red snapper. Some farm-raised catfish are lean.

Dried, Smoked and Salted Fish: Drying and smoking were common methods of preservation before refrigerators arrived in this steamy part of the world. Smoked herring or mackerel are inexpensive choices for many of these recipes. Herring is salted before being dried and smoked, so be sure to soak it for several hours before adding it to the sauce. You can also use smoked whiting, kippered herring, and more expensive varieties like smoked trout, haddock or smoked salmon. Salted fish such as cod (stockfish) and mackerel are common in West African cooking, and should also be soaked several hours before cooking to remove salt.

Ground Crayfish: This popular seasoning is made from small crustaceans, dried and ground to a powder. It has a fishy, pungent flavour that blends with a sauce to give it that real African taste. You can find African crayfish both as a powder or whole. Throw the whole ones in the food processor and grind them up yourself. If you can not get African crayfish, try a Spanish or Asian store for dried shrimp or fish sauce.

Oils

Palm Butter: This thick red paste is made from palm nuts which have been boiled, pounded to a pulp and strained. Canned palm butter can be purchased in many African food stores. It is used as a base for a seafood sauce.

Peanut Oil: The second most commonly used oil in African cooking, this versatile and widely available oil can stand up to anything from salad dressings to deep frying.

Red Palm Oil: This rich, red oil is a staple and necessity for real West African food. It is pressed from the fibrous flesh around the nut of the fruit of the oil palm, *Elaeis guineensis,* which has been cultivated in this part of the world for thousands of years. Palm oil, also known as manja or zomi, is used liberally in soups and sauces, yet because of the unique flavour and aroma the dishes are delicious rather than greasy and oily. Although it gets a bad reputation for being highly saturated, red palm oil is actually healthier than white palm oil. Red palm oil is about 50% saturated. It is very high in Vitamin A, and an important concentrated energy source. *White palm oil* is extracted from the palm kernel itself, and does not have the same deep red colour and flavour of red palm oil. White palm oil is often used in commercial baked products and cosmetics, and merely labeled "palm oil". It is about 80% saturated. Both types of oil are thick or even solid at room temperature, especially if you live in a cold climate. Red palm oil is available in African food stores. (See photo on page 127.)

Shea Butter: This fat is extracted from the nut of the shea tree of West Africa. The smooth-skinned nut is about the size of a walnut, and surrounded by a yellow or greenish black pulp. Shea butter is used to make margarine and chocolate. According to local lore the walls of the ancient Hausa city of Surame were built of mud mixed with Shea butter. The story goes that Kanta, the Fulani leader, ordered all conquered Hausa cities to come and help build the walls of Surame. Bida, Kano, Zaria, Ilorin, Bornu and Gwanja all arrived on time. However the people of Nupe were late, and as a punishment Kanta ordered that the mud for their portion of the wall be mixed with shea butter to make it extra hard.

Mai-maya tsuntsu ne in an juma sai ya tashi.

Juicy meat is like a bird, if you wait it will have flown.

Bibliography

Achebe, Chinua. *Things Fall Apart.* London: William Heinemann Ltd. 1958

Africa News Service. *The Africa News Cookbook.* New York: Viking, 1986

Bayley, Monica. *Black Africa Cookbook.* San Francisco: Determined Productions, Inc., 1971

Coyle, Patrick. *The World Encyclopedia of Food.* New York: Facts on File, 1982

Davidson, Basil. *Lost Cities of Africa.* Boston: Little, Brown, 1959

Ghana Nutrition and Cookery. Edinburgh: Thomas Nelson and Son, Ltd, 1960

Gisslen, Wayne. *Professional Cooking.* New York: John Wiley and Sons, 1995

Graf, Alfred Byrd. *Tropica Color Cyclopedia of Exotic Plants and Trees.* Roehrs Co, 1992

Grant, Rosamund. *Taste of Africa.* New York: Anness Publishing Ltd, 1995

Hahn, Emily. *Africa to Me.* New York: Doubleday, 1964

Hallet, Robert. *Africa to 1875.* Ann Arbor, Michigan: The University of Michigan Press, 1970

Hobben, S.J. and Kirk-Greene, A.H.M. *The Emirates of Northern Nigeria.* London: Oxford University Press, 1966

International Women's Club. *Recipes from the Crocodiles.* Nigeria: Baraka Press Ltd, 1981

Jahn, Jahnheinz. *Through African Doors.* Faber and Faber, 1964

July, Robert W. *A History of the African People.* Prospect Heights: Waveland Press, Inc, 1992

Newman, James L. *The Peopling of Africa.* Dexter, Michigan: Thomson-Shore, 1995

Niane, D.T. *Sundiata An Epic of Old Mali.* London: Longman Group Limited, 1979

Olaore, Ola. *Traditional African Cooking.* Slough: Foulsham, 1990

Oka, Monica Odinchezo. *Black Academy Cookbook.* Buffalo: Black Academy Press, 1972

Sandler, Bea. *The African Cookbook.* New York: Carol Publishing Group, 1994

Tannahill, Reay. *Food in History.* New York: Crown Trade Paperbacks, 1988

Van der Post, Laurens. *African Cooking.* New York: Time Life Books, 1970

Ward, Artemas. *The Encyclopedia of Food.* New York: Artemas Ward, 1923

Whitman, Joan and Simon, Dolores. *Recipes into Type.* New York: Harper Collins, 1993

Williams, Geoffrey. *African Designs from Traditional Sources.* New York: Dover, 1971

Wilson, Ellen Gibson. *A West African Cookbook.* New York: M. Evans, 1971

Acknowledgments

I am grateful to the following people for the generous donation of their time, advice and encouragement as they bravely tested these recipes.

Becky Seaman
Cathy L. Susa
Christine M. Christ
Debra F. Quinn
Debb Forster Wilson
Doug Cox
Faith Escudero
Jane Hopkins
Jo Smith
K. Laia Ogburn
Lavina Jackson
Mari Bendorfeanu
Michele LeFever Quinn
Sylvia Royer Taussig
Virginia M. Haney (Mrs. Paul Haney)

This book could not have been made if my father had not generously shared his photographs, library and knowledge of West Africa. Thanks to all the Hillcresters and other MKs who shared ideas and information on the internet. Finally, I want to thank my husband and kids for years of patiently eating West African dishes while I developed these recipes.

Yarda alheri baya ka dauke shi a gaba.
Throw happiness behind, you will pick it up in front.

List of Illustrations

Index